BEING IN CHRIST

That Christ may walk in us and dwell wholly in us, that he may reveal us whole in himself and himself whole in us.
St Andrew of Crete

If you and I are to live religious lives, it mustn't be that we talk a lot about religion, but that our manner of life is different.
Ludwig Wittgenstein

Peter Phillips

Being in Christ

A STUDY IN CHRISTOLOGY

the columba press

First published in 2013 by
the columba press
55A Spruce Avenue, Stillorgan Industrial Park,
Blackrock, Co. Dublin

Cover by Bill Bolger
Origination by The Columba Press
Printed by MPG Printgroup

ISBN 978 1 85607 852 8

For Andrew and Helen Williams
John and Barbara O'Neill
and their families
whose friendship has meant so much

Contents

Preface

One of the great privileges of being involved in the ministry of teaching is the opportunity this gives for learning. In many ways this study reaches back into my early days of secondary teaching at St Augustine's, Wythenshawe, and the Junior Seminary at Up Holland in Lancashire. Then when I moved on to Trinity and All Saints, Leeds, and Ushaw College, Durham, I was able to engage with older groups of students. In all these institutions I have been challenged again and again by stimulating conversations and questions: this is the real joy of teaching. In later years I have worked with groups, both as part of the formation course for deacons, as well as those wishing to deepen their understanding of the faith, in the diocese of Shrewsbury and elsewhere. It has been a great privilege to share some of this material over the years with the Auxiliaries of the Apostolate in Lourdes. I am really grateful to all those who have asked questions, and forced me to a continuing questioning.

Even as an undergraduate my enthusiasm for this subject was stimulated by the privilege of having been taught in Durham by the Revd Professor C. K. Barrett, the Revd Canon Dr John McHugh, the Revd Professor John Heywood Thomas, and the Revd Canon Professor H.E.W. Turner; I owe to them my warmest thanks, hoping that they will not be too disappointed at the use I have made of their teaching and generous personal support. I thank Fr David Roberts and Fr Adrian Graffy for their careful reading and comment on the manuscript, and my mother, Mary Phillips, for her most helpful suggestions. As always, I must thank Bishop Brian Noble for his warm support and encouragement as he celebrates fifty years of ministry in the church, and long suffering parishioners who have to put up with a rather preoccupied and, at times, cranky pastor.

Sections of this study appeared originally as part of the Christology Unit in an online version of the *Catholic Course in Religious Studies* published by Ushaw College; I am grateful to the College for allowing me to use material for which College authorities hold the copyright. I am also grateful to the editor of *New Blackfriars* for permission to use material which originally appeared in three articles in that journal:

'Schillebeeckx's Soteriological Agnosticism', *New Blackfriars*, February 1997, pp. 76–84.
'Seeing with Eyes of Faith: Schillebeeckx and the Resurrection of Jesus', *New Blackfriars*, May 1998, pp. 241–50.
'The Cross of Christ, Sacrifice and Sacred Violence', *New Blackfriars*, June, 2000, pp. 256–64.

Peter Phillips
The Feast of the Resurrection 2011

CHAPTER ONE

God has made him both Lord and Christ

First Encounters

Most of us have our first encounter with the wonder and mystery of Jesus Christ by way of other Christians. We are moved by what Christians stand for, and feel that what they hold to be true makes sense of this business we call living. The community of Christians is our first gospel. But soon we need to know more and we turn to the writings of the first communities of Christians as they tried to make sense of their own encounter with Christ, and the experiences which helped them to give shape to the New Testament. But this, too, cannot be a task undertaken in splendid isolation (2 Pet 1:20–21). We interpret the scriptures in the midst of a community of belief, stretching not only back in time to the first generation of disciples, but also amongst our contemporaries, from one end of the world to the other, wrestling with their varying insights and experiences as an encounter with Jesus Christ challenges them to engage with the world around them.

For John Henry Newman, the special privilege of the first generation of Christians was an encounter with Christ free of creeds and articles of faith. Peter, John, James, Martha, Mary; these were men and women who had met and talked with Jesus; they knew him. The disciples simply embodied their experience of Christ their Lord in the practice of discipleship. But Newman recognised a falling away from the immediacy of the apostolic age: right practice needs to be held in check by right belief. Catching up a phrase from the eschatological discourse of Matthew, Newman sets this understanding within the inevitability of the historical process by acknowledging 'a time when love grows cold' (Mt 24:12).[1] during which the immediacy

---

1. John Henry Newman, *University Sermons*, SPCK, London, 1970, p. 197.

of first love needs to be structured and channelled. With the advent of disagreement and heresy, the church is challenged to put its belief into words. This is a sad, but inevitable, necessity. Definitions tend to limit. Nevertheless the movement is not all one-way: right practice (orthopraxis) continues to challenge and modify right opinion (orthodoxy) just as much as expressions of faith determine how a Christian is to act. The two aspects of believing must be held together in a creative dynamic.

The earliest communities bear witness to a rich and varied pattern of Christological experimentation. The source for this was provided by the Hebrew scriptures. We cannot hope to come to any insight about the activity and person of Jesus, unless we set him firmly against the horizon of the Hebrew scriptures. The disciples' reflection on scripture did not create their experience, but it certainly allowed them to make sense of something that was not of their making. The Old Testament provides the language and categories for giving words, even shape, to such an experience. Sometimes such fragments allow further development, sometimes not, representing merely a false start, and coming to a dead end. The New Testament texts have already developed beyond these positions, preserving only fragmentary allusions to what has gone before. We lack sufficient evidence to construct a complete picture of the beliefs of individual communities, but careful work allows us to discover important clues to what had gone before.

Lord and Messiah
It is a quite remarkable fact that within about twenty years of a criminal's ignominious death on the gibbet of the cross, a group of strictly monotheistic Jews were proclaiming that this same man mediated God's final forgiveness, and stood at the threshold of the new age. Already in the earliest text contained in the New Testament, Paul's first letter to the community in Thessalonica, written about 50 CE, Jesus was being related to the mystery of God in the phrase 'God the Father and the Lord Jesus Christ' (1 Thess 1:1). It would be an interesting exercise to count just how many times this phrase and its alternatives are used in this short letter. Such an address is echoed in the conclusion of Peter's Pentecost sermon found in Acts 2:14–36: 'Therefore let

the entire house of Israel know with certainty that God has made him both Lord and Messiah [Christ]' (v. 36). Like the letter to the Thessalonians, this sermon is generally regarded as a good summary of the earliest Christian preaching. This is not a matter of a tradition changed and mythologised over generations, but a development which had taken place in living memory. There were still many alive who had known Jesus and had listened to him, or disagreed with him. Such men and women would surely have challenged an interpretation of Jesus they failed to recognise. The speed of Christological development in these early years is astounding.[2]

Writing to the community in Philippi a few years later, possibly as early as 56 CE, Paul quotes a hymn used in the Christian community, a text which probably dates back to an earlier period:

Phil 2:5–11	*Is 45:21–25*
Let the same mind be in you that was in Christ Jesus, who, though he was in the form of God, did not regard equality with God as something to be exploited, but emptied himself, taking the form of a slave, being born in human likeness. And being found in human form, he humbled himself and became obedient to the point of death – even death on a cross. Therefore God also highly exalted him and gave him the name that is above every name, so that at the name of Jesus	[There is no other god beside me, A righteous God and a Saviour; there is no one besides me … Turn to me and be saved, all the ends of the earth! For I am God and there is no other. By myself I have sworn, from my mouth has gone forth in righteousness a word that shall not return:]

2. See Martin Hengel, *The Son of God*, Fortress Press, 1976, p. 91.

every knee should bend, in heaven and on earth and under the earth, and every tongue should confess that Jesus Christ is Lord, to the glory of God the Father.	'To me every knee shall bow, every tongue shall swear.' Only in the LORD, it shall be said of me, Are righteousness and strength.

With breathtaking daring this pre-Pauline hymn develops an astonishing parallel between Isaiah's proclamation of God and Christ: every knee shall bow and every tongue shall now swear not to God himself, but in recognizing that Jesus Christ is Lord to the glory of God the Father. It is Karl-Joseph Kuschel's cautious conclusion that Paul's Christological legacy consists in the discovery of:

> A *kyrios* [Lord] alongside *theos* [God], the way in which the 'one God' and 'one Lord' belong together. This mystery drove the Jew Paul to the limits of his theological competence. His experience of Christ – beginning with the Damascus experience – led him to a unique experience of the depths of God as a result of which he could no longer understand the God and Father without Jesus the Son. It was an experience in which he dared to think not only of the depth of the lowliness of the crucified Nazarene, but also the depth of the origin and derivation of Christ 'from God' – more hinted at in quotation than explicitly developed.[3]

Perhaps the most significant factor contributing to this development is to be found in the community's worship. We are told that the earliest Jerusalem community, like their fellow Jews, gathered daily in the Temple, but also devoted themselves to the apostles' teaching and fellowship, to the breaking of bread and the prayers (Acts 2:42; see also Acts 2:46; 20:7, 11, 27:35; Lk 24:30, 35). Possibly we see here already early references to the celebration of Eucharist, which provided the primary focus for the prayer and discussion, enabling the community to

3. Karl-Joseph Kushel, *Born Before All Time? The Dispute over Christ's Origin*, SCM, London, 1992, p. 303.

enrich and deepen its understanding of the life, death and resurrection of Jesus the Christ.

Already in Paul's letter we see that the Greek word *Christos* has replaced the Hebrew *Messiah* ('anointed one', a designation of the king, or, perhaps later, priest); it is being used as a proper name, not a title. It is important to note that, although we are very familiar with the use of *Messiah/Christ* in our early Christian texts, and often suggest it is a title whose meaning is clearly defined in the Hebrew Scripture, this is not the case. Scholars are beginning to appreciate that first-century Palestinian–Judaism is in no sense monolithic, but a rich complex of disparate and often conflicting traditions.[4] The idea of the Messiah certainly occurs occasionally in the literature of Qumran and other contemporary material but does not stand out, nor is its meaning clearly defined. The Messiah is generally to be understood as a human agent of salvation, something still evident in the attitude of the first disciples. The word's prominence derives only from the fact that it is given a rather different meaning as the Christian texts unfold.

Jesus was understood by his first followers as the Christ/Messiah because he was the one who stood at the threshold of a new age and proclaimed the in-breaking of the reign of God. The expression 'reign of God', or its equivalents, is found throughout the gospels: 13 times in Mark; 13 times in Q, the passages common to Matthew and Luke; 25 times in Matthew's unique material; 6 times in texts found only in Luke; twice in John. Rather surprisingly it does not occur in the Hebrew scriptures, and only rarely in contemporary Jewish literature. We find the phrase occasionally used by Paul, but generally in passages which Paul could well have taken over from the traditional formulae of faith which he had inherited, such as 'for the kingdom of God is not food and drink but righteousness and peace and joy in the Holy Spirit' (Rom 14:17). It is a phrase which takes us to the lips of Jesus himself.[5]

---

4. See J.H. Charlesworth, 'From Jewish Messianology to Christian Christology, Some Caveats and Perspectives', in Neusner et al., *Judaisms and their Messiahs at the turn of the Christian Era*, Cambridge University Press, Cambridge, 1987, pp. 225–64.

5. John P. Meier, *A Marginal Jew*, vol. 2, Doubleday, New York & London, 1994, p. 238.

A Suggestive Ambiguity

There is an important and suggestive ambiguity about the title Lord, *kyrios* in Greek. It is found frequently in New Testament texts. It can function simply as a form of address to a superior: 'Mister', or 'Sir', we might say, as we find in the parable of the man with the fig tree (Lk 13:6–9). The gardener pleads with his master, 'Sir (*kyrie*) let it alone for one more year.' But this is also the word used to talk of God in the Greek version of the Hebrew scriptures, the Septuagint (LXX), and sometimes in the New

---

A note on the title YHWH in the Hebrew Scriptures

Ancient written Hebrew consists only of consonants, the vowels being introduced by the speaker. When Moses asks God his name at the incident of the Burning Bush, God replied, 'I AM WHAT I AM (*ehyeh asher ehyeh*) ... Thus you shall say I AM has sent me to you' (Ex 3:14). The Tetragrammaton (the four letters), YHWH in Hebrew, found in the next verse, was deemed too sacred to be uttered and it was never pronounced; indeed it was blasphemy to do so. In spoken Hebrew it was always replaced by *Adonai* (*Kyrios*, Lord). The *Mishnah*, an important rabbinic collection dating, in its present form, from about 200 CE, includes amongst a list of those who do not merit life after death: 'Abba Saul says, "Also: He who pronounces the divine Name as it is spelled out"' (Mishnah, Sanhedrin 11:1). When vowels were later added above and below the text, the vowels for *Adonai* were written around the consonants YHWH leading to the artificial hybrid $J_eH^oW_aH$, which is still sometimes used.

Traditionally, it has been the custom of the church to honour the sensitivities of our Jewish brothers and sisters by not pronouncing the name YHWH; the Lectionary follows this tradition, always replacing the Tetragrammaton with the word Lord. Unfortunately the *Jerusalem Bible*, first published in English by a team of scholars in 1966, broke with this tradition, and so have several modern hymns. Recently the Congregation for Divine Worship and Discipline of the Sacraments has instructed that Y_aHW_eH should not be vocalised, being replaced always by Lord or another appropriate circumlocution (see *The Tablet*, 23 August 2008).

Testament it clearly refers to God. Jesus, quoting Deuteronomy 6:13, is doing just that in his dismissal of Satan at the end of the temptation narrative (Mt 4:10): 'Worship the Lord your God, and serve only him.' Similarly Jesus' prayer to the Lord of the harvest refers to God (Mt 9:38). This form of address permits the New Testament authors to play on the changing meanings of the word, allowing the reader to move much closer to proclaiming Jesus' identity with God. There is no doubt that the Aramaic *Mari* or *maran(a)*, 'my lord', 'our lord' is embedded in earliest Palestinian Christianity.[6] We encounter the phrase in the closing verses of the New Testament: '"Surely I am coming soon." Amen, Come Lord, Jesus!' (Rev 22:20), and, in its Aramaic form, *marana tha* in 1 Cor 16:22.

Apart from passages in which they are quoting the Scriptures, Mark and Matthew speak directly of Jesus as Lord only once (Mk 11:3//Mt 21:3, Mark's account of preparations for the entry into Jerusalem before the Passion in which Jesus sends his disciples to bring a donkey and its colt: 'The Lord needs it.' Matthew rather incongruously includes a colt as well, revealing his misunderstanding of the Hebrew poetic doubling [*parallelismus membrorum*] of Zechariah 9:9). Jesus is recorded as being addressed as such rather more frequently by bystanders. Matthew, for example, develops Mark's protest of the disciples in the boat caught in a storm on the Lake of Galilee into a prayer to God for salvation.[7] No matter what the disciples thought at the time, the author of Matthew's gospel here addresses Jesus as Lord (Mk 4:38//Mt 8:25). Luke uses the expression much more often: 'when the Lord saw her, he had compassion for her ...' (Lk 7:13); 'after this the Lord appointed seventy others ...' (Lk 10:1). The process becomes even more pronounced in the Acts of the Apostles (Acts 5:14; 9:10), and in the New Testament letters. Lord is clearly one of Paul's preferred titles for Jesus, found 184 times in those letters which are accepted as authentically Pauline; the expression Son of God, in contrast, occurs only fifteen times in such letters. Here we are very close to what is probably the church's first creedal statement: 'Jesus is Lord.'

---

6. R.H. Fuller, *The Foundations of New Testament Christology*, Lutterworth, London, 1965, p. 154.
7. See below, pp. 57–9.

The Reign of God
It is unfortunate that our English Lectionary, and most of our New Testament translations, have opted for 'kingdom of God' as a translation of *basileia tou theou*, the underlying metaphor being determined by place: the place where God reigns; even heaven as opposed to earth, the place to which we hope to go after death. There is a certain loss of energy here. The American Lectionary is more successful, translating the expression as 'reign of God': the activity of God's reign unleashed upon the world. We encounter God more appropriately in activity, in verbs, rather than substantives, nouns. God is not the object of our devotion but is subject, the source and possibility of our acting in the world. As Augustine makes clear in his great work on the Trinity, God is not the end product of our love but is discovered as the one in whom we learn what it is to love another. In the loving of the other we find God:

> Let no one say 'I do not know what to love.' Let him love his brother or sister, and love that love; after all he knows the love he loves with better than the brother or sister he loves. There now, he can already have God better known to him than his brother or sister, certainly better known because more present, better known because more inward to him, better known because more sure. Embrace love which is God, and embrace God with love.[8]

This passage should be understood as the key for this whole study of Christ. Christ is not simply an object of belief for Christians. He is the encounter which sets us free for doing the work of Christians: 'the task of christology is in fact no other than to bring to expression what came to expression in Jesus himself.'[9] The best christology is a lived experience, our belief a way of being human. It is a living out of the Lordship of Christ.

Jesus' message is: 'Repent, for the reign of God has come near' (Mt 3:2; 4:17, see Mk 1:15). There is a certain ambiguity in the Greek text here. In the first place, repent (*metanoeite*) is not an invitation simply to say sorry for past ways, but calls to a change

8. St Augustine, *The Trinity*, introduction, translation and notes Edmund Hill OP, *The Works of St Augustine*, part I, vol. 5, New City Press, New York, 1991, bk viii, § 12.
9. Gerhard Ebeling, *Word and Faith*, SCM, London, 1984, p. 304.

of heart, a change of direction, a turning topsy-turvy of our lives. The expression 'come near' (*ēggiken*) is similarly misleading and open to being translated in two ways: 'the reign of God has come near [in the teaching and activity of Jesus]', or 'The reign of God is [chronologically] near at hand.' Certainly the text of Lk 17:21 ('the reign of God is in your midst') inclines towards the first interpretation. Jesus taught his disciples to pray for the unleashing of God's reign, the doing of his will here on earth, not only in heaven (Mt 6:10). Some New Testament scholars, following the groundbreaking studies, Johannes Weiss's *Jesus' Proclamation of the Kingdom of God* (1892), and Albert Schweitzer's *The Quest of the Historical Jesus* (1906; Eng. ed. 1910), set Jesus clearly in the context of the proclamation of the end of the world. He is understood as an eschatological figure (Greek: *eschaton*, 'the last or end time'), who saw himself to be the one who was to proclaim the final in-breaking of the reign of God and the end of the world as it had been experienced.

The gospels offer some evidence for the suggestion that certainly at first the disciples did not understand Jesus' proclamation of the reign of God but looked to the appearance of God's reign as an earthly intervention. The poignant words of the disciples on their encountering a stranger on the way home to Emmaus are telling: 'We had hoped that he was the one to redeem Israel' (Lk 24:21). The question was still being mooted in the days after the resurrection: 'Lord, is this the time when you will restore the kingdom to Israel?' (Acts 1:6). The hot-headed brothers, James and John, 'the sons of thunder' as they were nicknamed by Jesus (*Boanerges*, Mk 3:17, see Lk 9:51–56) certainly were anticipating an earthly kingdom when they asked Jesus whether they could share his rule (Mk 10:35–45), a remark delicately re-attributed to their mother by Matthew to spare their blushes as they became well-known figures in the early community (Mt 20:20). The disciples' early misunderstanding cannot be interpreted as suggesting that the good news of the gospel has nothing to do with politics. Although the good news remains far richer than liberation from political oppression, the reign of God is about engaging with this world, not escaping from it. The proclamation of the reign of God brings liberation and healing for society at a deeper level, but God's reign challenges all regimes, all institutions and all societies which diminish what it means to be fully human. As disciples, we are called to contribute to the transforming of the earth, and the transforming of society, that they may the better be sacraments of God's reign.

The Inauguration of God's Reign

It is true that the earliest communities certainly looked in the first place to an expected immediate coming (*parousia*) of the reign of God. Paul had to warn the Thessalonians not to give up work and live in idleness in the expectation of the *parousia*, but to go on working (2 Thess 3:6–13). Mk 9:1 ('Truly, I tell you, there are some standing here who will not taste death until they see that the kingdom of God has come with power'), one of the most difficult verses to interpret, suggests that Jesus himself expected that God's reign would break in at any moment. The author of the gospel seems concerned about its meaning, putting it in a position where it might be interpreted simply as an introduction to the narrative of the transfiguration. Mk 13:32–37, in turn, seems to be an attempt to allay fears that God's reign had not arrived as expected, and there are similar verses throughout the New Testament.

The earliest New Testament christologies look to a future coming of God's reign. Although Luke's Acts of the Apostles is a relatively late work, possibly written in Greece or Syria in the 80s of the Common Era, it appears to contain fragments of much earlier material. Peter's sermons (Acts 2:14–36; 3:17–26) offer clues to one of the earliest christologies in the New Testament: a tantalising glimpse of one of the most primitive interpretations of the person of Jesus. It is tempting to accept John Robinson's suggestion that the most primitive attempt towards a systematic understanding of the person of Christ is that found in the speech of Acts 3:12–26.[10] Here we have, according to John Robinson, 'a first tentative and embryonic christology of the early Church, as it struggled to give expression to the tumultuous implications of what had happened in Jerusalem in these last days'.[11] This is a view that regards Jesus as the 'forerunner of the Christ he is to

---

10. John A.T. Robinson, 'The Most Primitive Christology of All?', *Journal of Theological Studies*, 7 (1956), pp. 177–89.
11. Art. cit., pp. 183–4.

be',[12] not yet Messiah, though, without doubt, destined to become so.

Deeply rooted in the theology of the Hebrew scriptures such a christology represents the questioning of a community looking forward to that 'act which would inaugurate the Messianic rule of God and vindicate him as the Christ'.[13] It is Robinson's contention that the earliest community had yet to identify this divine vindication with the cross and resurrection of Jesus. This is a theme taken up also by Rudolf Bultmann who points out that the earliest Christian communities did not understand the coming of the Son of Man as a return, but simply as an arrival, an advent (*parousia*). The use of the expression Son of Man plays a critical role in the development of New Testament christology and is a theme which we shall explore in the next chapter. Suffice it to say at this point, a christology focused entirely on a future coming was soon to be superseded: Bultmann points out that it was not until the second century writer, Justin, that we find the contrast between 'first' and 'second' coming of Christ (Justin, *Dialogues*, 14.8, 40.4), as well as the idea of his 'coming back' (Justin, *Dialogues*, 118.2).[14]

The example gives a hint of the diversity of theologies in the earliest proclamation and offers a pointer towards a christology which appears even more primitive than the normative second coming christology, although it clearly represents a stage on the way to this. It underlines just how complex is the thinking of the earliest communities regarding the Easter experience and its 'tumultuous implications'. The terms for this debate were not ready to hand and had to be wrested from encounter not only with the risen Lord himself but with material provided by the scriptures.

In his later letters Paul uses the word *parousia* in a non-technical sense in a manner that might have been used by anyone in the Greek-speaking world ('when I come [*parousia*] to you again' [Phil 1:26]; 'I rejoice at the coming [*parousia*] of Stephanus, and Fortunatus and Achaius' [1 Cor 15:16]). In contrast, the earlier letter of Paul, more dominated by the pressure of the expected

---

12. Art. cit., p. 181.
13. Art. cit., p. 185.
14. Rudolf Bultmann, *Theology of the New Testament*, vol. 1, SCM, London, 1971, p. 29.

immediate in-breaking of the reign of God, seem to use Christ's *parousia* as a technical term for Christ's relationship with this new world and his return ('For what is our hope or joy or crown of boasting before our Lord Jesus at his coming? [*parousia*] [1 Thess 2:19; see also, 3:13, 4:15, 5:23]). There is evidence in the pre-Pauline communities that Christians were increasingly identifying the earthly life and activity of Jesus with the future Messiah and Son of Man. His words and deeds were being interpreted as intimately involved with the coming reign of God, something Paul tended to ignore. This was indeed the reason for the writing of the gospels.

As time went by the focus increasingly shifted to the present. Jesus himself and his earthly ministry are now regarded as integral to the identity of the Messiah. Jesus is not simply Lord of the future, but Lord of the present community. The communities of the church live out their mission during the times between the defining events of Easter and the second coming; the present times are understood as being determined by the Lordship of Christ. The teaching Jesus first gave to his Jewish audience in the fields of Palestine is now to be reinterpreted as teaching for the community of the church. This is something exemplified in the Sermon on the Mount (Mt 5–7). As Jacques Pohier comments so appropriately: 'the Beatitudes and the Sermon on the Mount are not the map of life in another world but the map of another life in this world.'[15]

The Alsatian scholar, Oscar Cullmann, tempers the two extremes: the reign of God is already upon us with the coming of Jesus and yet, at the same time, looks to a future completion. Writing shortly after the end of the Second World War he used the analogy of the difference between D-Day and VE Day.[16] After the success of the D-Day landings the allied victory was assured, but there were serious and costly operations to go through, and many more deaths and injury, before the final victory, with the surrender of Berlin to the allied forces. Jesus' return is better not understood to be immediate, but immanent, an event determining and challenging all our values, an opening to a new and exciting world. The peculiar 'in-betweenness' of Christian

---

15. Jacques Pohier, *God in Fragments*, SCM, London, 1985, p. 101.
16. Oscar Cullmann, *Christ and Time*, third edition, SCM, London, 1967, pp. xix, 84.

existence determines not merely its chronology, but, more importantly, its very character.[17] As disciples, we are at every moment to be open to the great horizons of God's reign, rather than cowering within the narrow confines of our limitations.

Divine Wisdom

We need now to turn to a rather different theme: the great christological hymns found in the letters to the Colossians (Col 1:15–20) and Hebrews (Heb 1:1–4) and the prologue to John's gospel (John 1:1–18). The first two letters written possibly in the 60s of the Common Era, but most probably about twenty years later, and John's gospel written rather later still, represent examples of differing second- or third-generation communities, which though written very much in a Greek milieu, look back to a clearly identifiable Hebrew tradition which personifies divine wisdom, often regarding it as the source of God's creating activity. The best example of this is to be found in the book of Proverbs:

> Does not wisdom (*hokmah*) call,
> and does not understanding raise her voice? ...
> The LORD created me at the beginning of his work,
> the first of his acts of long ago.
> Ages ago I was set up,
> at the first, before the beginning of the earth.
> When there were no depths I was brought forth,
> when there were no springs abounding with water.
> Before the mountains had been shaped,
> before the hills, I was brought forth –
> when he had not yet made the earth and fields,
> or the world's first bits of soil.
> When he established the heavens, I was there,
> when he drew a circle on the face of the deep,
> when he made firm the skies above,
> when he established the fountains of the deep,
> when he assigned to the sea its limit,
> so that the waters might not transgress his command,
> when he marked out the foundations of the earth,
> then I was beside him, like a master worker;
> [the word for 'master worker', can also be interpreted 'little child']

---

17. See Rudolf Bultmann, *Theology of the New Testament*, vol. 2, SCM, London, 1958, p. 170.

I was his daily delight,
rejoicing before him always,
rejoicing in his inhabited world
and delighting in the human race.
(Prov 8:1, 22–31; see also Ps 104; Job 38–42)

The Hebrew *hokmah* (Greek *sophia*) in this passage is beginning to be understood as having an identity in relation to God
but possessing also both a creating and saving role (see Prov
3:19; Wis 7:22, 27). Wisdom is the agent of God's creative activity
in the universe. Monotheism, though still strictly held, becomes
rather more nuanced in later Judaism than is often recognised.
This is something which comes increasingly to the fore in
Second Temple Judaism.[18] Wisdom is regarded more and more
as a personal being standing by the side of God. God's wisdom
is also identified with the Torah which is also given personal
characteristics. God's word (Hebrew *dabar*, Greek *logos*) also
plays an increasingly important role. A word found frequently
in the Hebrew scriptures, it is active, expressing God's creative
command: 'He sent out his word and healed them' (Ps 107:20);
'he sends out his command to the earth; his word runs swiftly'
(Ps 147:15). The Alexandrian Jewish philosopher, Philo, a contemporary of Jesus, developed a philosophical position which
linked the Stoic–Platonic theories of the *Logos* with Hebrew
speculation about creation and thus produced a fertile soil for
the crossing of Hebrew and Hellenistic thought. The systematic
ambiguity of the word *Logos* which drew together the Hebrew
Wisdom, the Greek principle of rationality in the cosmos, as
well as the Christian 'Word made flesh' (Jn 1:1–18) provided a
powerful focus for biblical thinking.

Already glimpsed in Mark, when the people remark about
Jesus' visit to the synagogue in his home village: 'Where did this
man get all this? What is this wisdom that has been given to him?
What deeds of power are being done by his hands!' (Mk 6:2), we
find a deepening association of Jesus with Wisdom in parts of
the sayings source which is common to Matthew and Luke, often
called Q (see, for example, Mt 11:19//Lk 7:35; Mt 12:42//Lk

---

18. See Margaret Barker, *The Great Angel: A Study of Israel's Second God*, SPCK,
London, 1992.

11:31). The hymns of Colossians and Hebrews and the prologue of John's gospel bring this process to a conclusion. They are not concerned with mythological speculation but celebrate the exaltation of Christ at the end times (eschatology) now reflected back to the beginning of all time (protology) to proclaim Christ's priority over creation (Colossians), his role as saviour (Hebrews), and as revelation of God's redemptive love (John).

Although, as we have seen, Paul focuses the great hymn of Philippians on Jesus' death on the cross (Phil 2:8, see above), John's prologue proclaims his birth (Jn 1:14). These christological hymns tend to be more abstract and have little place for the details of Jesus' earthly life. It was John's achievement to unite these two strands in his gospel. As Raymond Brown notes: 'indeed, only in John is the term "God" applied to all phases of the career of the Word: the pre-existent Word (1:1), the incarnate Word (1:18), and the risen Jesus (20:28)',[19] thus promoting the 'uniquely high christology' of John contrasted even with the Pauline and post-Pauline material marking a transition from the hymn genre with its Wisdom model (Phil 2:6–7; Col 1:15–16; John 1:1–18) to gospel genre, which describes the words and deeds of Jesus.

The more fully developed, incarnational christology of John was indeed carried into the early church and taken up by a theology shaped in the cultural setting of the Graeco–Roman world.[20] It was also read back into earlier christologies. We are accustomed to identify the christologies worked out in terms of Jesus' virginal conception in the opening chapters of Matthew and Luke with the pre-existence/incarnation christology of John's gospel. Raymond Brown suggests we should discriminate between the two christologies a little more carefully: the christology which lies behind the virginal conception of Christ contrasts with both adoptionist and incarnational christologies.

19. Raymond Brown, *The Community of the Beloved Disciple*, Paulist Press, 1979, p. 46.
20. 'The intrinsic necessity of a rapprochement between biblical faith and Greek inquiry' was the true theme of Benedict XVI's now rather infamous lecture at Regensburg (*The Tablet*, 23 September 2006, pp. 10–12). I would beg to disagree: Greek thought, while providing brilliant insights for theological discourse, moves in a very different world from the dynamic of biblical categories, which still have a lot to offer in our attempts to think out what it means to be a disciple of the Lord in different cultural settings.

The two strands of thought became integrated only later:

> It is no accident that John never speaks of the 'begetting' of Jesus, for Jesus simply is ('I am'). I stress the difference between conception Christology and pre-existence christology, because Christian theology soon harmonised the two ideas, so that the pre-existent Word of God was described as taking flesh (John) in the womb of the virgin Mary (Matthew and Luke). The virginal conception was no longer seen as a begetting of God's Son but as the incarnation of God's Son, and that became orthodox doctrine.[21]

It is out of this context that the Western way of doing theology has developed. Before we turn in Chapter Five to examine how this worked out, we must look at some more New Testament attempts to make sense of the Lordship of Christ.

---

21. Raymond Brown, *The Birth of the Messiah*, Doubleday, London and New York, 1988, pp. 141–2.

CHAPTER TWO

One like a Son of Man

A Conundrum

The phrase Son of Man offers something of a conundrum for New Testament scholars. In Greek, the phrase makes little sense (*ho huios tou anthrōpou*) so that there can be no doubt that it belongs to the Hebrew (*ben ādhām*) and Aramaic (*bar nāŝā*) roots of the New Testament. The phrase occurs in the Psalms (e.g. Ps 8:4), and the prophet Ezekiel (e.g. 2:1), as well as in second century Christian writings (*Epistle to Barnabas* 12:10; Ignatius, *Letter to the Ephesians* 20:2), referring simply to a human being, or to the humanity of Christ in contrast to his divinity. In the New Testament this is not the case: it is a phrase expressive of a divine mandate. The phrase occurs twice in Revelation (1:13; 14:14), once in Acts (7:56), never in Paul, but frequently in the four gospels: fourteen times in Mark; thirty times in Matthew; twenty-five times in Luke; and thirteen in John. With the possible exception of Mark 2:10, one instance in the gospels where the phrase Son of Man is not on the lips of Jesus, we find the phrase always occurring on the lips of Jesus himself.

Moreover, the expression does not belong simply to one strand of the gospel narratives, but is found throughout the four gospel texts. In John's gospel the phrase has a slightly different resonance, so, for the sake of simplicity, we shall put these examples to one side. Its use can usefully, but not altogether successfully, be divided into three groups: one illustrating Jesus' present, earthly authority; another consisting of sayings pointing to a future in-breaking of the reign of God; and finally, sayings referring to Jesus' suffering and death. The first group can be illustrated by sayings such as 'Foxes have holes, and birds of the air have nests; but the Son of Man has nowhere to lay his head' (Mt 8:20//Lk 9:58), or 'the Sabbath was made for humankind, and not humankind for the Sabbath; so the Son of

Man is lord even of the Sabbath' (Mk 2:27–28). In a number of sayings Jesus is recorded as talking of his forthcoming passion and death in terms of the Son of Man: 'The Son of Man is to be betrayed into human hands, and they will kill him, and three days after being killed, he will rise again' (Mk 9:31//Mt 17:22//Lk 9.44 [with considerable omissions in the latter]). Mk 10:45 hints at an interpretation of his death, which we shall examine later: 'For the Son of Man came not to be served but to serve, and give his life as a ransom for many.' The final group look to the future, where Jesus is quoted as talking about coming glory or vindication: 'Those who are ashamed of me and of my words in this adulterous and sinful generation, of them the Son of Man will also be ashamed when he comes in glory' (Mk 8:38); 'When they persecute you in one town, flee to the next; for truly I tell you, you will not have gone through all the towns of Israel before the Son of Man comes (Mt 10:23).

More ink has been spilt exploring this expression than on any other in the New Testament, and scholars have apparently come to little consensus on the matter. Ernst Käsemann, writing in 1953, claims that the phrase was not used at all by Jesus himself, but had its origin in the thought of the post-Easter period.[1] A.J.B. Higgins argues that only the use of the phrase pointing to the future glory of the Son of Man as advocate or judge can be attributed to the earthly Jesus.[2] Geza Vermes denies that the expression in any way represents a title used in Judaism, arguing that it represented an idiomatic way in Aramaic in which a teacher/ prophet might refer to himself in the third person.[3] We might remember that Vermes has an additional agenda, wishing to disassociate Jesus from any eschatological context, presenting Jesus as merely an itinerant healer. Barnabas Lindars, following Vermes, argues that only the present sayings and passion sayings can be authentic, the future sayings being the product of early Christian reflection.[4]

We are left trying to make out how we might make our way through these disagreements. Of course, we can accept that not

---

1. Ernst Käsemann, *Essays on New Testament Themes*, SCM, London, 1981, p. 43.
2. A.J.B. Higgins, *Jesus and the Son of Man*, Lutterworth, London, 1964.
3. Geza Vermes, *Jesus the Jew*, Fontana, London, 1973.
4. Barnabas Lindars, *Jesus and the Son of Man*, SPCK, London, 1983.

all examples of the phrase may go back to Jesus himself; some might have been added, some deleted. It will be noticed that in some of the examples I have given above, it is not always clear that Jesus identifies himself with a figure 'the Son of Man'. This seems to be most clearly the case in the passion sayings, but in Mk 8:38 and Mt 10:23 there is room for doubt, as there is also in Mk 2:10. This is suggestive. As the phrase is so well represented in so many different areas of Jesus' activity, it seems inappropriate to exclude any group wholesale. Of course it would also be inappropriate to argue that all the examples of the phrase have come from the lips of Jesus; some have undoubtedly been introduced as a result of the editorial activity of the early church, just as some have been lost.

In comparing parallel texts occurring in different gospels we find at times a seeming development: Mk 8:38 ('Those who are ashamed of me and of my words in this adulterous and sinful generation, of them the Son of Man will also be ashamed when he comes in his glory') is reworked in Mt 10:32 ('Everyone therefore who acknowledges me before others, I will also acknowledge before my Father in heaven; but whoever denies me before others, I will deny before my Father in heaven'). Here Matthew clearly identifies Jesus and the Son of Man. Perhaps here we have a further example of the move from the earliest theology of a coming Messiah, not yet identified explicitly with the person of Jesus, and a slightly later theology which marks the increasing identification of the earthly Jesus with that coming figure, something I have explored briefly in the first chapter.

Most scholars compound the confusion by interpreting the expression Son of Man as used in the gospels in terms of a title associated with an eschatological figure as it seems to be in the pseudepigraphal Similitudes of Enoch (1 Enoch 37–71) and IV Ezra 13 (a text occurring only in the appendix to the Vulgate). Both these texts are now thought to be late first century writings, and thus too late to have contributed to the formation of the New Testament.[5] Nevertheless they offer useful examples of parallel interpretations of the phrase to that found in the New Testament. 1 Enoch does hint at a development of the phrase

---

5. C.F.D. Moule, 'Neglected features in the problem of the Son of Man', in *Essays in New Testament Interpretation*, Cambridge, 1982, p. 76–7.

tending towards personification as a heavenly being; IV Ezra still regards the expression primarily as a metaphor.

One like a Son of Man in Daniel 7:13

Apart from these texts, there is virtually no evidence of the Son of Man being used as a title in the period we are dealing with. The expression has its origin in the book of Daniel:

> As I watched in the night visions
> I saw one like a human being
> (*kebar 'enāš*: N.B. not *the* Son of Man, but *something like* a Son of Man)
> coming with the clouds of heaven.
> And he came to the Ancient One
> and was presented before him.
> To him was given dominion, and glory and kingship,
> that all peoples, nations and languages
> should serve him.
> His dominion is an everlasting dominion
> that shall not pass away,
> and his kingship is one that shall never be destroyed.
> (*Daniel 7:13–14*).

It is important to appreciate the context in which this passage occurs. This is a prophetic dream offering consolation to God's suffering people, and promising vindication and healing after a period of persecution. The persecuting nations are represented by four monstrous beasts but these will receive judgement in God's court while God's faithful people, 'the holy ones of the Most High' (Dan 7:22, 27), will be vindicated. The 'one like a human being' (Dan 7:13) can thus be related to the 'holy ones' (Dan 7:22, 27), and represents them before God, just as the four monsters represent the persecuting nations. The figure is a metaphor for God's vindication of his persecuted ones. If this is the case, Jesus' answer to the High Priest's question 'Are you the Messiah, the Son of the Blessed One?': 'I am; and "you will see the Son of Man seated at the right hand of the Power", and "coming with the clouds of heaven".' (Mk 14:61–62) represents not precisely a prophecy about the appearance of a heavenly figure, but, after the manner of IV Ezra, a powerful metaphor for God's vindication of Jesus, his message, and those whom he represents. But the vindication of Jesus is also in the humiliation and exaltation of the cross: the proclamation of Jesus as the one whom God has appointed as vindicator. The judged is acquitted and becomes, in turn, the judge.

C.F.D. Moule points out that a similar vindication scene to that of Daniel 7 is echoed in the setting of Psalm 110:

> The LORD says to my lord, 'Sit at my right hand until I make your enemies your footstool.' (Ps 110:1; see also Ps 2 and Ps 8)[6]

This psalm, quoted more often in the New Testament than any other passage in the Hebrew scriptures, and found embedded in different traditions underlying the New Testament,[7] is central for the shaping of the christology of the earliest communities. It offers important clues to the earliest Christian interpretation of the Easter experience as vindication and exaltation of Christ, passing from death to life and sitting at the right hand of the Father. Norman Perrin makes a strong case for identifying the way in which the first generation of Christians worked out their theology in a manner akin to, but not identical with, what we find in other groups within second Temple Judaism. This is in terms of a Christian *pesher* tradition.[8]

Perrin suggests that the starting point of our exploration should be the second part of Peter's speech in Acts 2:14–36. Here the Messianic rule of Christ is contrasted to the earthly rule of David, exalting Christ as heavenly Lord. There is no question of raising the matter of Jesus' Davidic descent. In what could well be an incomplete fragment preserved from a longer, lost original in Mark 12:35–37 Jesus blocks a probing and intrusive question by again challenging the necessity of the Davidic descent of

---

6. C.F.D. Moule, *The Phenomenon of the New Testament*, SCM, London, 1967, p. 83.
7. Notably Peter's Pentecost sermon, Acts 2:34 (the significance of which is explored brilliantly in Barnabas Lindars, *New Testament Apologetic*, SCM, 1961, pp. 36–51), as well as Mk 12:36, 1 Cor 15:25, Heb 1:3, 13. Luke's own 'development and rethinking of eschatology in an individualistic direction' is explored in C.K. Barrett, 'Stephen and the Son of Man', in *Apophoreta. Festschrift für Ernst Haenchen (Beihefte zur ZNW 30)*, ed. W. Eltester, Berlin, 1964, pp. 32–8.
8. *Pesher* is simply Hebrew for 'interpretation'. It represents a Jewish method of scriptural interpretation which applies the words of scripture in seeking to make sense of the present situation of the community in its struggle against opposition. Norman Perrin, *Rediscovering the Teaching of Jesus*, SCM, 1967, pp. 173–85. See also, Norman Perrin, 'Mark 14.62: the end product of a Christian Pesher Tradition?', *New Testament Studies*, 12 (January 1966), pp. 150–5.

the Messiah. The heavenly lordship of Christ is greater than any title David could claim for himself repeating the argument of Acts 2:34.

More specifically, Perrin offers further evidence which suggests that we can trace three remnants of a tradition of interpretation which is based on Dan 7:13. The first of these again starts with Ps 110:1. Here, as I have already suggested, we see the victim vindicated, out of which derives the additional notion of exaltation, coming to God rather than coming from God:

> 'you will see the Son of Man seated at the right hand of the Power.' (Mk 14:62a)

Secondly, Perrin argues for a passion apologetic starting from crucifixion rather than the resurrection and which uses Zech 12:10:

> And I will pour out a spirit of compassion and supplication on the house of David and the inhabitants of Jerusalem, so that when they look on the one whom they have pierced, they shall mourn for him, as one mourns for any only child, and weep bitterly over him, as one weeps over a firstborn.

This is picked up in Mt 24:30:

> Then the sign of the Son of Man will appear in heaven, and then all the tribes of the earth will mourn, and they will see 'the Son of Man coming on the clouds of heaven' with power and great glory.

It also underlies John 19:37: 'They will look on the one whom they have pierced'.

Thirdly, we have a further use of this passage which brings the notion of *parousia* to the fore, putting more and more emphasis on the expectation of the second coming, coming from God rather than going to God: 'Then they will see "the Son of Man coming in clouds" with great power and glory' (Mk 13:26); and 'coming with the clouds of heaven' (Mk 14:62b). Perrin concludes:

> It seems, then, that in the first place Ps 110:1 has been conflated with Dan 7:13 without change to the fundamental meaning that Jesus is declared to be Messiah by his Exaltation. But the allusion to Dan 7:13 has later (but still in the pre-Markan phase) exerted an increasing influence, resulting in the expansion of the text to convey a new meaning.[9]

---

9. Barnabas Lindars, *New Testament Apologetic*, SCM, London, 1961, p. 49.

Redemptive Suffering

The phrase Son of Man became particularly important for the Palestinian church because tentatively it allowed a way of interpreting Christ's redemptive suffering, something the term Messiah was unable to express. But the way from vindicator and judge to redeemer is not easily mapped out and there is surprisingly little evidence to be found in the earliest layers of New Testament. It was only later that the image of the suffering servant of Isaiah 53 began to play an important part in the church's understanding of her Saviour:

> The righteous sufferer is a familiar figure; so is the righteous sufferer vindicated; but the unrighteous oppressor rescued from his evil ways through that vindication – was anything so illogical ever heard of or hinted at before. So far as one can see, the answer is no, nor yet after – unless it be in that moving passage in the Pentateuch where it is implied that Moses' self-surrender might somehow help to restore the guilty people (Ex 32:32) ... Jesus only occasionally *spoke* of his *representative* work; when he did, it is questionable whether he drew on the words of Isaiah 53. But his work *was* redemptive. It was his person rather than his words or his quotations which brought this home.[10]

A witness to the events surrounding the crucifixion of Jesus on a hill outside Jerusalem in the early first century would not have been able to identify any aspect of what was going on as sacrifice. Here was simply a judicial murder performed with some cynicism by the Roman administration of a difficult province. For the Temple administration Jesus' death was understood as a matter of an expediency, pointedly ironised by the author of John's gospel: 'You do not understand that it is better for you to have one man die for the people than to have the whole nation destroyed' (Jn 11:50). There seems little doubt, on the other hand, that the gospels, as well as Paul, place the death of Jesus firmly within an interpretative framework provided by the sacrifice of Passover; this, in turn, leads to the early claim that Christ's death is to be understood in relation to the forgiveness of sins. This theme is already present in the primitive creedal statement preserved in 1 Cor 15:3, which Paul seems to

---

10. C.F.D. Moule, *The Phenomenon of the New Testament*, SCM, London, 1967, pp. 95, 99.

have inherited from Palestinian Christians, and most probably from the Jerusalem church itself.[11]

Edward Schillebeeckx challenges this understanding by refusing to acknowledge a soteriological motivation in the most primitive form of the synoptic passion narrative: 'No saving function is as yet ascribed to them as being propitiation for sin.'[12] Schillebeeckx rightly suggests that sacrificial language of expiation, which has God alone for its subject, slips all too easily into talk of the priestly offering of propitiation for sin to God. It is not inevitable that it should do so. Schillebeeckx is careful to acknowledge that the Old Testament refrains from a complete identification of the sin-offering with what he considers to be the priest's task of 'bringing about expiation "for someone"'. He seeks to establish a clear distinction between the forgiveness of sins (which can have only God for its subject) and expiation of sins (the subject of which, he suggests, remains at least ambiguous, and which at times is not necessarily divine): 'The forgiveness of sins and the expiation of sins involved two different semantic fields', the former belonging to the 'juristic priestly acquittal from sin, rather than to the New Testament experience of salvation in Jesus from God'.[13] Schillebeeckx refuses to recognise that expiatory language can appropriately be used to proclaim God's healing forgiveness.

This refusal provides the grounds for Schillebeeckx's rejection of sacrificial language as an appropriate way of talking of Jesus' death. It seems that he is unable to isolate sacrificial language from what he regards as inevitable overtones of propitiation. Schillebeeckx seems unprepared to make the distinction (which is just about universally accepted in English) between propitiation and expiation. The former has God for its object and is understood in terms of a human attempt to avert divine wrath while the latter has God for its subject. 1 John 4:10 makes it clear that to understand Jesus as an offering for sin (*hilasmos*) does not mean that he renders a hostile God friendly but that it

---

11. See Martin Hengel, *The Atonement*, SCM, London, 1981, pp. 37–9.
12. Edward Schillebeeckx, *Jesus An Experiment in Christology*, Collins, London, 1979, p. 284.
13. Edward Schillebeeckx, *Christ: The Christian Experience in the Modern World*, SCM, London, 1980, pp. 485–90.

is because God loves us that he *sends* his Son as an *hilasmos* to take away our sin.[14] Bearing this distinction in mind, we can rightly understand, and accept wholeheartedly, Schillebeeckx's abhorrence of the language of propitiation. This is a point he confirms in his *Interim Report*:

> It is precisely when the message and conduct of Jesus which led to his death are ignored that the saving significance of this death is obscured. Jesus' death is the intrinsic historical consequence of the radicalism of both his message and his way of life, which demonstrated that all master–servant relationships are incompatible with the kingdom of God. The death of Jesus is the historical expression of the unconditional character of his proclamation and life-style in the face of which the fatal consequences for his own life faded completely into the background. The death of Jesus was suffering through and for others as the unconditional endorsement of a practice of doing good and opposing evil and suffering. Thus the life and death of Jesus must be seen as a single whole. Furthermore it was not God, 'who abominates human sacrifices', who brought Jesus to the cross. That was done by human beings, who removed Jesus from the scene because they felt he was a threat to their status.[15]

The language of propitiation is indeed completely 'foreign to Biblical usage',[16] as C.H. Dodd argued as long ago as 1932 in his important commentary on Romans, and very few modern New Testament scholars would disagree with his interpretation.

The Language of Sacrifice

Inappropriate propitiatory overtones, easily to be associated with the concept of sacrifice, should not lead us to dismiss the language of sacrifice too hastily from a discussion of Jesus'

---

14. I owe this point to the kindness of my colleague, Bernard Robinson.
15. Edward Schillebeeckx, *Interim Report on the Books Jesus and Christ*, SCM, 1980, p. 133.
16. C.H. Dodd, *The Epistle of Paul to the Romans*, Fontana, 1970, p. 78. The Team, under the direction of Dodd, which produced the New English Bible translates Rom 8:3 'by sending his own son ... as a sacrifice for sin', reserving 'to deal with sin' as an alternative reading. While it is correct that the Greek expression here (*peri harmatias*) was sometimes used in the LXX as a translation of the Hebrew 'sin-offering' (*asham*), the meaning is much better conveyed by the phrase 'to deal with sin'. This was acknowledged in the text of the Revised English Bible. See also, C.K. Barrett, *The Epistle to the Romans*, Adam and Charles Black, 1971, pp. 77, 156.

death. The point can be developed further by exploring the tendency to read Mk 10:45 by way of Isaiah 53:10 which is evident in the work of such eminent New Testament scholars as Joachim Jeremias.[17] Such an identification of these two texts leads the reader to see Jesus in terms of the sin-offering. This is something that must be examined with care. C. K. Barrett differs from Jeremias in basing his argument on the Septuagint text rather than on the Hebrew or Aramaic text. In a meticulous examination of the background of Mk 10:45, Barrett makes it clear that it is incorrect to read the Greek text of Mark in the context of the Septuagint text of the fourth of the so-called 'servant songs' (Is 52:13; 53:12). Barrett's discussion makes clear that 'the linguistic connection between ransom (*lytron*) in Mk 10:45 and Isaiah 53 is non-existent: *lytron* is not found in the Septuagint as a translation for *asham*.'[18] The Hebrew word found in Isaiah 53:10 includes the notion of guilt-offering which is absent from the Greek word. Morna Hooker develops this theme by arguing the case that the noun *lytron* itself is not used in the Septuagint as a sacrificial term but only in the technical sense of 'purchase money'.[19] It is the verb *lytroō* that, though often still retaining the technical sense, is sometimes found both in the Pentateuch and in the prophetic writings in a figurative sense which refers to God's redemption of his people either from their bondage in Egypt or from Exile in the East:

> It should be noted that the primary thought in this conception of God as Redeemer is one of historical activity by Yahweh … Nor is there any emphasis on the payment of an equivalent, the original meaning of ransom: it is enough that Yahweh acts decisively; the result, not the method of his action is what is important … The emphasis is on death and deliverance rather than on sin and suffering. The words are thus in keeping with the spirit of the first half of the first century AD, which as we have seen, was still concerned with deliverance from foreign oppression, rather than with theories of atonement as such.[20]

---

17. See Jeremias, *New Testament Theology*, vol. 1, p. 292ff, where Jeremias argues that we should accept a reading of *lytron* which does not exclude the notion of substitutionary offering (*asham*).

18. C.K. Barrett, 'The Background of Mark 10:45' in *New Testament Essays: Studies in Memory of T. W. Manson*, ed. A.J.B. Higgins, 1959, pp. 1–18, esp. p. 7.

19. Morna Hooker, *Jesus and the Servant*, SPCK, 1959, esp. pp. 74–9; *The Son of Man in Mark*, SPCK, 1967, pp. 144–7.

20. Morna Hooker, *Jesus and the Servant*, pp. 76, 78.

Professor Barrett finds the true linguistic background of *lytron* (ransom) in the Rabbinic use of *kapparah* (expiation), and suggests a more cogent general context for the verse by relating it to the Greek text of Maccabees. The last of the seven brothers martyred because of his refusal to eat pig-flesh makes this prayer, 'I, like my brothers, give up body and soul for our fathers' laws, calling on God to show favour to our nation soon, and to make thee acknowledge, in torment and plagues, that he alone is God, and to let the Almighty's wrath, justly fallen on the whole of our nation, end in me and my brothers' (2 Macc 7:37–38).[21]

Further weight to this reading can be offered by two texts, one from the close of the Jewish period and another amongst the earliest of non-biblical Christian sources. These are the Fourth Book of Maccabees and the letters of Ignatius of Antioch. 4 Maccabees takes the form of a sermon probably addressed to an audience in Alexandria somewhere between 63 BC and AD 38, that is 'within two generations before or one generation after the Christian era'.[22] In this text Eleazar's dying prayer from the flames of the pyre is depicted in the following way: 'Thou, O God, knowest that though I might save myself I am dying by fiery torments for thy Law. Be merciful unto thy people, and let our punishment be a satisfaction on their behalf. Make my blood their purification, and take my soul to ransom (*antipsycon*) their souls' (4 Macc 6:27–29). Reflecting on the horror of the torture and death of Eleazar and his family, the author understands them as 'a ransom for our nation's sin' and a means of expiation (*hilasterion*) (4 Macc 17:22). The letters of Ignatius put us in touch with a similar world. Just a short time later than 4 Maccabees, if we retain the traditional early date for the letters of Ignatius, we find the author entreating the Ephesians in the words, 'I am a ransom for you.'[23] Lightfoot commenting on the meaning of ransom, 'a life offered for a life', refers to the two passages of 4 Maccabees I have already mentioned and suggests that 'the direct idea of vicarious *death* is more or less obliterated, and (that) the idea of devotion to and affection for another stands out

21. Moffat's translation in R.H. Charles, *The Apocrypha and Pseudepigrapha of the Old Testament*, vol. 1, Oxford, 1913.
22. Townshend, in R.H. Charles, *The Apocrypha and Pseudepigrapha of the Old Testament*, vol. 2, Oxford, 1913, p. 654.
23. Ignatius, Ephesians 21; see also Smyrnaeans 10; Polycarp 2.

prominently'.[24] Ignatius understands this offering of his own life as an echo of Christ's offering praying that he might be allowed to be 'an imitator of the passion of my God'.[25]

Expiation in Exodus 32:30–32

Barrett makes a strong claim that we should look to Ex 32:30–32 for the biblical roots of the term:[26]

> On the next day Moses said to the people, 'You have sinned a great sin. But now I will go up to the LORD; perhaps I can make atonement for your sin.' So Moses returned to the LORD and said, 'Alas, this people has sinned a great sin; they have made for themselves gods of gold. But now, if you will only forgive their sin – but if not, blot me out of the book that you have written.

In these verses we see Moses' preparedness to stand in the breech and make atonement for the people's sin incurred by setting up the Golden Calf. Here, Barrett suggests, we can identify the roots of a rich tradition. For Schillebeeckx, Moses is to be understood as the archetype for the eschatological prophet and Barrett suggests that it is precisely in this tradition that we find a correct understanding of the Hebrew noun *kapparah* (expiation), a word still used in modern Hebrew as a conventional expression of commitment and love. Like many of the Old Testament martyrs, Jesus is expressing 'his devotion – a devotion that would shrink from no sacrifice – to the true welfare of his people … the *amme ha'ares*, the great mass of the people as opposed to (though not in this case necessarily excluding) the pious groups'.[27] If this verse has its origin in an expression that initially includes no immediate reference to the death of the speaker, Jesus' commitment to the outcast and his challenge to the security of the reigning powers might suggest that this might lead inevitably to death and that his death be understood as the clearest expression of such a commitment:

---

24. Lightfoot, *The Apostolic Fathers*, part 2, vol. 2, Macmillan, 1889, pp. 87–8.
25. Ignatius, Romans 6.
26. C.K. Barrett, 'Mark 10:45: A Ransom for Many', in *New Testament Essays*, SPCK, 1972, pp. 20–6. See also C.K. Barrett, *Jesus and the Gospel Tradition*, SPCK, 1967, pp. 45–52, 67.
27. Barrett, 'Mark 10.45: A Ransom for Many', p. 24.

Once the connection with the death of Jesus was made the saying would inevitably be exposed to theological polishing. Comparison of Mark 10:41–5 with the partial parallel in Luke 22:25–7 not only shows that such polishing has taken place but also that the two gospels contain independent traditions. Each has some features that are more primitive than the other. The theological development was not all on Hellenistic soil ... The purpose of the present note is not to deny the existence of this theological development of the tradition, but to suggest a possible starting-point, itself of both historical and theological significance, for the tradition. If Jesus did not say, I am (or, my soul is) a *kapparah* for all Israel, he acted on this principle, and this service to the mass of his people occasioned, and at the same time provided the interpretation of his death.[28]

Professor Barrett's suggestion that we should understand *lytron* (ransom) by way of the Rabbinic *kapparah* (expiation) suggests that we should be rather more cautious in disassociating the notion of sacrifice from Christ's death too swiftly. Schillebeeckx is clearly correct in arguing against an understanding of sacrifice as propitiation. As we have seen, however, sacrifice has a much wider range of reference in the Jewish world to which Christ belongs. Such contemporary understanding is far from alien to Schillebeeckx's reading of the life and ministry of Christ. His starting point, in a manner akin to the position we have elaborated here, rests in the tradition of an eschatological prophet rooted in an understanding of Moses as a suffering mediator. At the same time, our current discussion allows us to say significantly more about the soteriological significance of the death of Jesus than Schillebeeckx will allow. Using texts such as these we can conclude that a sacrificial interpretation of this death is at least consonant with, and indeed not unlikely to have its origin in, the life and ministry of Jesus himself.

This extended examination of the use the earliest communities made of the phrase Son of Man allows us to begin hesitatingly to find words to express the dark and costly nature of God's passionate love for us as it is worked out in the mystery of the crucifixion. This is something touched on in Donald MacKinnon's remarkable aside, made during a lecture: 'Was

---

28. Barrett, 'Mark 10.45: A Ransom for Many', p. 25.

there that which Jesus alone could do, in the manner in which it had to be done, that was of such moment for humanity that the risk was justified, the cost well spent?'[29] Here we are made at one again with the ground of our existence (at-one-ment, a word coined in the early sixteenth century, and found in the works of St Thomas More, is one of the few technical theological terms the English language has contributed to the language of theology). We shall return to this theme in chapter seven. Now, however, we shall need to discuss at some greater depth the theme of vindication, exaltation and resurrection in the New Testament, and the various developments of christology which grew out of this.

---

29. Cited in a letter from Sebastian Moore to the Editor of *New Blackfriars*, *New Blackfriars*, October 2000, p. 448.

CHAPTER THREE

Vindication, Exaltation and Resurrection

Relating Resurrection and Ascension
There seem to be two contrasting movements in the period of
the formation of the New Testament and earliest church communities. On the one hand we see an attempt to conflate accounts of resurrection and ascension; on the other, an attempt to
separate them. The post-resurrection gospel texts represent a
rather unsteady compromise between these two positions: John
20:29 hinting at Jesus' conferring of the Spirit (what we now understand as Pentecost) on the evening of the resurrection; the
Luke of Acts introducing a period of forty days before an identifiable ascension (Acts 1:3); Luke's gospel is more uncertain,
seemingly like John, putting Christ's withdrawal from his disciples and being carried up to heaven (Lk 24:29) on the day of
resurrection itself. We can also note two different approaches to
the ascension, one guided by the more ambiguous, theological
language of exaltation (Mk 16:19; 1 Tim 3:16 'was received up
into heaven/glory'; Phil 2:9 'highly exalted'), the other by the
more straightforward language of apparently physical movement (Acts 1:11 'going'; John 7:33 'I go'; Lk 24:51 'parted', with a
possible allusion to 2 Kgs 2:11 (LXX) 'separated', used of Elijah
and Elisha). This dynamic can be represented by the interplay of
four key terms: exaltation, resurrection, ascension, *parousia*. The
earliest accounts seem not to have achieved stable form: sometimes one of these terms is to the fore, sometimes another.

Accepting the Easter experience as given, we need to ask
ourselves whether we are to regard the resurrection idea as the
oldest and original interpretation of this experience, or whether
we can argue that there were other interpretations. Attempts to
do justice to this question form the roots of the community's

christology, fragments of which have been preserved in the New Testament and related texts. Carrying out this task leads to a complex journey both into the literature of the Hebrew scriptures and their contemporary interpretation in the communities of Judaeo–Christianity. A similar play of essential meaning and symbolism comes to the fore as we explore the post-resurrection narratives of the gospels. We cannot do justice to the New Testament picture unless we acknowledge it to be far more complex than a mere consideration of the post-resurrection texts in themselves. We cannot hope to offer any insight into Jesus' resurrection if we deal with it as a discrete event. It must be understood firmly against the horizon of the Hebrew scriptures.

Resurrection, ascension, the conferring of the Spirit, exaltation to the right hand of the Father, *parousia*, are rooted in the rich and subtle tapestry of Second Temple Judaism. In the New Testament narratives, it is Luke who most clearly separates these inter-related images and we follow him appropriately in structuring our liturgical celebration and our appropriation of the experience of new life which we experience in Christ. All these concepts find their identity in the underlying theme of vindication, central to the Hebrew scriptures as I have suggested in discussing the meaning of the key phrase, Son of Man. Vindication, I suggest, is the primary biblical category by which we interpret the Easter experience. Resurrection is secondary: it is the way in which God's vindication is expressed and experienced in the New Testament narratives.

What is probably one of the earliest references to the resurrection is again to be found in Paul's first letter to the Thessalonians:

> For the people of those regions report about us what kind of welcome we had among you, and how you turned to God from idols, to serve a living and true God, and to wait for his Son from heaven, whom he raised from the dead – Jesus, who rescues us from the wrath that is coming (1 Thess 1:9–10).

Both Xavier Léon-Dufour and Edward Schillebeeckx point to this text, together with 1 Thess 4:14, as perhaps the earliest references to the Easter experience.[1] In these texts we have resurrection linked to a future coming, but not necessarily to an immediate post-resurrection appearance.

For Schillebeeckx the experience of the resurrection must be treated as independent of, and prior to, the accounts of the appearance and empty tomb narratives of the gospels.[2] Such accounts inevitably fail to do justice to the event itself. It is the underlying experience of encounter with the risen Christ, only later to be teased out in 'concrete and materialising terms' in the appearance and empty tomb narratives of the gospels that remains primary. These original experiences bear witness to 'a transcendent Christ who is revealed rather than observed ... an object that was perceived by faith rather than by sight'.[3] The narratives of empty tomb and post-resurrection appearance are thus to be thought of as the expression of, rather than the origin of, Easter faith; they are narratives in which the church recognises and affirms its experience of the risen Lord. It is in this encounter with the risen Lord, an encounter renewed through the ages in the community of belief, that men and women discover forgiveness and new meaning. This is an experience of salvation that is both very personal and also communal. Here Christians of each generation bear witness to their belief in the resurrection and in doing so attest the same experience as the apostles.

Differing Trajectories

Some insight into the underlying factors giving shape to the way in which the experience of the resurrection came to be expressed is afforded by a fascinating study of the first hundred years of Christianity by James M. Robinson.[4] Robinson argues that the formation of the New Testament belongs to a period 'strung on trajectories that lead not only from the pre-Pauline confession of 1 Cor 15:3–5 to the Apostles' Creed of the second

1. Xavier Léon-Dufour, *Resurrection and the Message of Easter*, Holt, Rinehart & Winston, 1974, p. 13; Edward Schillebeeckx, *Jesus An Experiment in Christology*, Collins, 1979, p. 346. I acknowledge the influence throughout this chapter of Edward Schillebeeckx's fine study.
2. Schillebeeckx, *Jesus*, p. 332–4, 354.
3. Peter Carnley, *The Structure of Resurrection Belief*, Oxford, 1987, p. 200.
4. James M. Robinson, 'Jesus from Easter to Valentinus (or to the Apostles Creed)', *Journal of Biblical Literature*, 101, 1 (1982), pp. 5–37.

century, but also from Easter "enthusiasm" to second-century Gnosticism';[5] Raymond Brown has argued similarly in his excellent study of the formation of the Johannine corpus.[6] Neither the position later understood to be heretical, nor that later accepted as orthodox, simply preserves the tradition without alteration. Robinson, drawing on a wide range of New Testament texts, makes a good case for arguing that the New Testament contains considerable evidence to suggest that the earliest tradition understands the resurrected Christ as a luminous, heavenly body.[7] Such a position was naturally a boon to those intent on arguing for a gnostic, anti-materialist interpretation; orthodoxy, in turn, reacted by increasingly emphasising the fleshly reality of the risen Lord. James Robinson concludes:

> Thus although orthodoxy and heresy could on occasion accommodate themselves to language actually developed to implement the emphasis of the other alternative, by and large they divided the Pauline doctrine of luminous bodiliness between them; orthodoxy defended the bodiliness by replacing luminousness with fleshiness, heresy exploited the luminousness by replacing bodiliness with spiritualness.[8]

In view of this, we could suggest that the earliest interpretation of the resurrection might well have been expressed in the language of exaltation and ascent, rather than of physical resuscitation.

Resurrection and Exaltation

The earliest tradition understands resurrection and exaltation as two aspects of the one eschatological event. This pattern of death and exaltation is seen in the early hymns preserved in Philippians 2:6–9 and 1 Tim 3:16, as well as in Mark 14:62:

---

5. Robinson, art. cit., p. 6. Gnosticism (Greek *gnōsis*, knowledge) is an insidious and curious muddle of Eastern religious ideas, mixed with Greek thought. Though it pre-dates Christianity, it was strong in the first centuries of our era, and Christianity found it necessary to define itself over against various Gnostic systems. Gnosticism proclaimed a strong dualism between matter and spirit, the former being evil, the latter good: the task of the soul being to find liberation from its ties to the cosmos by a spiritual liberation, escaping the thrall of evil variously by rigorous asceticism or by unlimited licence.

6. Raymond Brown, *The Community of the Beloved Disciple*, Paulist Press, 1979.

7. Robinson, art. cit., pp. 7–16.

8. Robinson, art. cit., p. 17.

'You will see the Son of Man seated at the right hand of the Power,' and 'coming with the clouds of heaven.'

Luke 24:26 ('Was it not necessary that the Messiah should suffer these things and then enter into his glory?') and 46 ('Thus it is written, that the Messiah is to suffer and to rise from the dead on the third day') seem to suggest that exaltation and resurrection may be used interchangeably to describe what happens after Jesus' death, so, too, does Mt 28:16ff.[9] In other passages in this same chapter Luke commits himself to a much more physical account of the risen body of the Lord, a body which could be touched (Lk 24:39) and could even consume food (Lk 24:43).

I have already shown just how important a part Psalm 110:1 plays in expressing the New Testament understanding of the exaltation of Christ. Peter's sermon in Acts 2:14–36, one of the early sources incorporated in the Acts of the Apostles by Luke, draws out the difference between resurrection and exaltation by introducing, apparently for the first time, Ps 16:10 ('for you will not abandon my soul to Hades, or let your Holy One experience corruption') as a text specifically marking out the resurrection. We can argue that at the roots of the tradition lies an objective encounter with the risen Lord which only later, as a result of pressure from the debate with gnosticism, came necessarily to be defined in increasingly materialistic terms. Luke–Acts represents just the beginnings of a process which, while rightly insisting on the reality of the risen Lord, seems to be drifting into a literalness which is increasingly less than helpful: Jesus' risen life is spelt out in terms more physical than metaphysical, more akin to resuscitation than resurrection.

Seeing the Lord

Another early account of Jesus' post-resurrection appearance is the passage in Paul's first letter to the Corinthians, which takes us back to the traditional formula to which Paul could well have been introduced when, visiting Peter and James in Jerusalem, he returned to the public eye three years after his conversion (Gal

---

9. Gerard O'Collins, *The Easter Jesus*, Darton Longman and Todd (DLT), 1973, p. 51, in his discussion of these passages, suggests the exaltation theme is a later interpretation of an earlier resurrection tradition. I would be rather more hesitant in arguing this.

1:18). We have here a tradition which belongs already to the earliest period of the Jerusalem community, a mere six to eight years after the events to which Paul is referring. Paul tells us the risen Christ appeared (*ophthe*) to Cephas (1 Cor 15:5). An echo of the same formula could well underlie Lk 24:34 ('The Lord has risen indeed, and he has appeared to Simon!'). Paul makes it clear that he is differentiating the appearance of Jesus to Peter from something which ought better to be described in the language of vision: he is talking about visionary experience in 2 Cor 12 and this seems to be a very different sort of experience. *Ophthe* (he was seen, he appeared), is the aorist passive of the Greek verb *horaō* (to see). The verb functions in rather the same way as the noun 'Lord', which we have already examined in Chapter One. Taken by itself, the biblical use of the aorist passive *ophthe* remains ambiguous: grammatically it can be understood as referring equally to an encounter with the resuscitated Lazarus, destined to die once more, or the risen Christ, who once and for all has broken the chains of death.

The importance of the discussion of *ophthe* lies in the fact that it is firmly rooted in the context of the language and concepts shaped by the world of the Hebrew scriptures as is related to accounts of God's revealing of himself. This is the verb we find in the Septuagint translation of the angel's appearance to Moses at the Burning Bush (Ex 3:2); Ex 34:10 talks of 'seeing (*opsetai*) the work of God'; Isaiah talks of seeing the glory of the Lord:

> Every valley shall be lifted up,
> And every mountain and hill laid low;
> The uneven ground shall become level,
> And the rough places a plain.
> Then the glory of the Lord shall be revealed (*ophthesetai*),
> And all peoples shall see (*opsetai*) it together,
> For the mouth of the Lord has spoken.
> (Is 40:4–5; see also 26:10, 35:2)

Isaiah, in another passage familiar from Handel's Messiah, tells us of God's future manifestation:

> Arise, shine; for your light has come,
> And the glory of the Lord has risen upon you.
> For darkness shall cover the earth,
> And thick darkness the peoples;

But the Lord will arise upon you,
And his glory will appear (*ophthesetai*) over you.
(Is 60:1–2)

In passages such as these the German scholar, Michaelis, comments, 'It is impossible to think in terms of sense perception, but one can also speak of spiritual perception and personal experience only in the sense of seeing as the receiving of the revelation of God in his *doxa* [glory].'[10] His discussion of this passage continues, 'The real reference here is to revealing presence rather than to visibility,'[11] the emphasis lying on the one who makes his presence felt rather than on the one who sees. This is particularly the case with the construction which we find in relation to the resurrection accounts: *ophthe* with the dative.[12]

To these passages we might add the short hymn preserved in 1 Tim 3:16), which is of particular interest:

He was revealed in flesh,
vindicated in spirit,
seen (*ophthe*) by angels / messengers,[13]
proclaimed among Gentiles,
believed in throughout the world.

The emphasis here, as J.N.D. Kelly suggests in his commentary on the passage, lies on Christ's triumphant vindication. He suggests such a passage should be linked to Phil 2:9, Col 2:15 and Heb 1:6.[14] One of the most powerful expressions of this theme, though the text appears not to be to the fore in the New Testament, is that found in the book of Job:

For I know that my Redeemer[15] lives,
And that at the last he will stand upon the earth;
And after my skin has been thus destroyed,

---

10. Wilhelm Michaelis, '*horaō*' in Gerhard Kittel, *Theological Dictionary of the New Testament*, vol. 5, Erdmans, London, 1967, pp. 315–82, passage cited from p. 326. See also Fergus Kerr, 'Paul's Experience: Sighting or Theophany', *New Blackfriars*, July 1977, pp. 304–13.
11. Michaelis, art. cit., p. 334.
12. Michaelis, art. cit., p. 358.
13. For the translation 'messengers' see Luis Alonso Schokel, *Nueva Biblia Espnola* (1975).
14. J.N.D. Kelly, *The Pastoral Epistles*, Adam & Charles Black, London, 1963, p. 90.
15. NRSV margin: 'Vindicator'; the *Jerusalem Bible*, rather more brutally translates, 'Avenger'.

Then in my flesh I shall see God
Who I shall see on my side,
And my eyes shall behold and not another. (Job 19:25–27)

Like Job it is the task of those who profess to be disciples of the
Lord to live out the fact that death and death-dealing experiences are not the end. This is not to trivialise evil, nor to seek to
explain it. It is demanded only that we confront it.

The Transformation of Earthly Existence

We must talk of Christ's resurrection in bodily terms in so far as
it says something about the transformation of earthly existence.
As humans we are embodied, part of the stuff of the universe.[16]
In the resurrection of Jesus, there is not only a promise, but the
foretaste of the life to come. The disciples' encounter with their
risen Lord makes this clear: there is both continuity with what
has gone before, but also a startling discontinuity. An encounter
with the risen Lord is an experience of the very threshold of the
new creation. His is a transforming presence. The Easter experience demands an engagement with the world not a flight from
it. Different ages seek different ways of avoiding this truth. The
besetting error of gnosticism lies in demanding that we look to
escape from the messy continuum of human living. As Luke's
second ascension narrative warns the disciples, they are not to
stand gazing up into heaven but to stay in the city (Acts 1:1–14).
Paul's insistence that the disciple must not avoid the rigours of
work has the same import (1 Thess 3:6–13). A materialistic reading of the resurrection suggests a different escape route: the
risen Lord becomes increasingly regarded as part of the continuum of human history, an object of human enquiry. But Christ,
in his resurrection, remains Subject, Lord of history, present not
past. The new life which the resurrection promises is not appro-
priated merely by looking back and weighing the evidence,
but by an encounter with the risen One, who comes to meet us
on the road of our own engagement with human suffering and
injustice. The disciple is called daily to conversion.

---

16. I have touched on this theme in 'Bonebound Spirituality', *New Blackfriars*,
    June 1990, pp. 297–303.

Interpreting the Resurrection Narratives

Neither epistles nor the canonical gospels describe the resurrection itself. Not everyone saw Jesus after the resurrection. The texts suggest that Christ appeared not indiscriminately, but to Peter, to particular groups. He appeared only to witnesses, those who had been with him as he journeyed towards Jerusalem (these are the criteria Peter insists on for the election of a replacement for Judas [Acts 1:21]). Paul seems to be something of an exception here, not having been a witness to Jesus' earthly life and ministry. The gospels make it clear that we are not talking about the resuscitation of a body – like Lazarus, for instance (Jn 11). Lazarus would die again in the course of time. Jesus would not. He is beyond the reins of death. The gospels suggest that there is something odd about his body: it seems no longer determined by constraints of the dimensions of space and place and time. If we were to ask whether the resurrected body of Jesus could be photographed, it might be appropriate to claim that we would not be at all sure of the answer.

The problematic nature of the resurrection texts is not just the conclusion of modern interpretation; it is something integral to the gospel texts themselves. Interestingly, Paul in warning the congregation gathered in Corinth that questions like 'How are the dead raised?', and 'With what kind of body do they come?' (1 Cor 15:35), are stupid questions, doesn't refer them back to Christ's resurrection. These are questions for which we have not the language to fashion adequate responses.

In tackling any of these texts we can be a little more certain of what they are saying about the theological meaning than about the physical detail of what actually occurred. We have made problems for ourselves in that much reflection on the resurrection reads the gospels primarily in terms of historical narrative rather than in terms of theology. In insisting on the historical reality of the risen Lord we seem to be seduced into a literalness which is none too helpful. This is a process which started very early on, even in the period which shaped the gospels themselves. In doing this, we refuse to read the gospels as gospel. The gospel texts themselves cannot be evaluated merely as descriptions of an event (whatever that might mean) but only as part of a whole, shaped by layers of interpretation.

Nevertheless we still need to ask about the status of state-ments referring to Jesus' manner of existence after death. We have some idea what 'crucified under Pontius Pilate' means: it is a historical statement in the same way as 'Caesar crossed the Rubicon' is a historical statement. As Karl Barth reminds us, Pilate's inclusion into the Creed affirms the fact that God has ir-revocably entered into the warp and weft of human history.[17] We have some idea what sort of statement 'he sits at the right hand of the Father' is: this is clearly a metaphorical statement – God has no hands. 'Our spatial standards are not appropriate for the different mode of the resurrection reality.'[18]

Scholars suggest that the accounts of the appearances of Jesus and the accounts of the empty tomb belong to separate traditions and that the empty tomb accounts are much the later of the two blocks of tradition, stories to reinforce the fact that Jesus appeared to the disciples. Paul seems to differ completely from the gospels in having no record of an empty tomb tradi-tion. The lack of certainty regarding the historicity of the empty tomb narratives suggests that we must set the story aside in considering the evidence for the resurrection.[19] Having said this, however, it is important to acknowledge that 'later' is not always 'of less significance' in the matter of forming historical judgements. Perhaps the German theologian, Paul Althaus, overstates that matter in claiming that the proclamation of the resurrection 'could not have been maintained in Jerusalem for a single day, for a single hour, if the emptiness of the tomb had not been established as a fact for all concerned',[20] but he has a point. An empty tomb certainly proves nothing but it is surely not without significance that no body was ever produced by Jew or Roman: evidence of a rotting corpse would have scotched the

---

17. See, for example *Dogmatics in Outline*, SCM, 1966, pp. 108–13.
18. Wolfart Pannenberg, *The Apostles Creed*, SCM, 1972, p. 124.
19. We must not overlook the fact that the empty tomb narratives have proved the starting point for profound reflection. See, for example, Rowan Williams, 'Between the Cherubim: The Empty Tomb and the Empty Throne', in Gavin D'Costa, ed., *Resurrection Reconsidered*, Oneworld Publications, 1996, pp. 87–101; Francis Watson, '"He is not here": Towards a theology of the empty tomb' in Stephen Barton & Graham Stanton, eds, *Resurrection*, SPCK, 1994, pp. 95–107.
20. Paul Althaus, *Die Wahrheit des kirchlichen Osterglaubens*, p. 22f, cited in Wolfart Pannenberg, *Jesus God and Man*, SCM, 1968, p. 100.

resurrection story once and for all. Both non-believers and believers seem to be familiar with the fact of an empty tomb.
Matthew reminds us of a piece of Jewish propaganda which argues that the disciples had smuggled the body away 'and this
story is still told among the Jews to this day' (Mt 28:15).

In the same way, in considering the narratives of the appearances of the risen Lord, we cannot simply argue that the later
accounts should be discounted. Pierre Benoit, in his painstaking
study of the passion and resurrection accounts, suggests that the
Johannine account 'although it was composed later ... in its earlier strata preserves memories that are older even than those of
the synoptics'.[21] Nevertheless it is evident that other elements
are beginning to intrude themselves into the later narratives.
They become more and more complex with more and more
emphasis on the physical state of the risen Christ; they develop
themes which are precious to the life of the early Christian community. Luke in his gospel seems to put all the appearances of
the risen Christ on the same event-filled day of the resurrection
before 'he withdrew from them and was carried up to heaven'
(Lk 24:50). John likewise has a completely different 'time scale'
which hints at the conferring of the Spirit on the evening of the
day of resurrection (Jn 20:29). It is in the Acts of the Apostles that
Luke introduces a period of forty days between the resurrection
and ascension leading to the conferring of the Holy Spirit at the
time of the Jewish celebration of the corn harvest on the feast of
Weeks, or Pentecost.

The way in which we generally interpret the resurrection
seems to focus on inference, on weighing the evidence. We bring
into prominence the later stories and the apparent detail pre-
sented in the gospels while ignoring the earliest tradition: Paul's
unembroidered comments recording Christ's appearance,
Mark's account of the resurrection which has no record of appearances at all. The resurrection remains veiled in mystery; the
tomb is found empty; Jesus appears to the disciples on a number
of occasions in differing situations. Is our belief a matter of
working out whether we think the disciples are telling the
truth, or not? Our experience of the risen Lord, it is claimed, is

---

21. Pierre Benoit, *The Passion and Resurrection of Jesus Christ*, DLT, 1969, p. 259.

different from that of the first disciples. They saw him; we haven't. Contemporary interpretation of the New Testament texts shows that it is not quite as simple as this.

To give an adequate account of the resurrection it is important to maintain that the disciples experienced something that was not of their making but, at the same time, that they made sense of it. The resurrection is not something that we accept because it can be inferred, worked out from first principles, or perhaps remembered on good authority, but it is experienced as a present and determining reality for the community of the church. Christ is risen, is the song of Christians. My belief rests not on private judgement but reflects the belief of the Christian community. It depends on God: it is not constituted merely by hearsay. It does not depend on my ability to sift the evidence, although it remains intimately bound up with what Donald MacKinnon points to as the 'explosive intellectual force'[22] of Jesus' life and ministry. Jesus could have done and said different things. There is no necessity which demands that the Father should manifest his vindication by way of the resurrection of the Son. It is revelation in history, not merely as history. God can surprise. In relation to the Cross the resurrection is a new act of God, as Barth has it: 'Judgement is judgement. Death is death. End is end.' And then comes a further intervention: God's free act of grace.[23]

Resurrection as Vindication

Vindication, in the Hebrew scriptures, remains both God's promise and the people's hope. In Christ the dynamic is changed. We are drawn into a necessary interplay between past, present and future. We must read Christ's life against the horizon of the Hebrew scriptures and as a foretaste of God's promised future. God's future vindication is experienced as something at the same time already accomplished and yet not fulfilled. Christ is the 'firstborn within a large family' (Rom 8:29), 'the first fruits of those who have died' (1 Cor 15:20).

---

22. Donald MacKinnon, 'Faith and Reason in the Philosophy of Religion', in *Philosophy, History and Civilisation*, eds David Boucher, James Connelly and Terry Modood, University of Wales Press, 1995, p. 86.

23. Karl Barth, *Church Dogmatics* IV. I, T&T Clark, Edinburgh, 1956, p. 290, pp. 304–9.

Christ's death and resurrection did not issue in the immediacy of the *parousia*, as many expected, but in its immanence, as that which determines and characterises every moment of existence.

To talk of resurrection in terms of vindication means two things, and a third follows. The resurrection is a vindication of what God stands for: that God is a loving God, a God who remains true to his promises. It is a vindication of what Jesus stands for: that what Jesus said and did, as he travelled from Galilee to Jerusalem, was for us and for our salvation. It follows from this that God's twofold vindication is intimately related to the uniqueness of Jesus' physical existence as a particular person living within the constraints of a particular time, the first century of our era, and a particular place, Galilee and the Roman province of Judaea. Christopher Rowland makes an important point in arguing that resurrection faith, as opposed to, for example, concentration on the immortality of the soul, or a stress on exaltation, brings with it an inescapable political agenda. Christians must look to this world and its transformation: 'resurrection will not permit the abandonment of the hope of the transforming power of God's justice in history.'[24] With Christ we have entered into the highly-charged period of the Last Days.

Reflecting on the Resurrection Narratives themselves
The four great narratives of the passion draw us as one under the shadow of the Cross. They overlap and come together in a way that is unique in the gospels. And then a sunburst: the narrative breaks into a myriad fragments. There is no way the resurrection accounts can be brought together to form a coherent and continuous narrative. They are not the same sort of gospel narratives as those which have gone before.

The Marcan account is stark in its simplicity:

> When the Sabbath was over, Mary Magdalene, and Mary the mother of James, and Salome brought spices, so that they might go and anoint him. And very early on the first day of the week, when the sun had risen, they went to the tomb. They had been saying to one another, 'Who will roll away the stone for us from

---

24. Christopher Rowland, 'Interpreting the Resurrection', in Paul Avis, ed., *The Resurrection of Jesus Christ*, DLT, London, 1993, p. 79.

the entrance to the tomb?' When they looked up, they saw that the stone which was very large, had already been rolled back. As they entered the tomb, they saw a young man, dressed in a white robe, sitting on the right side; and they were alarmed. But he said to them, 'Do not be alarmed; you are looking for Jesus of Nazareth, who was crucified. He has been raised; he is not here. Look there is the place they laid him. But go, tell his disciples and Peter that he is going ahead of you to Galilee; there you will see him just as he told you.' So they went out and fled from the tomb, for terror and amazement had seized them ... (Mk 16:1–8)

We can certainly take this literally, of course: it happened to be Sunday, it happened to be early in the morning at about sunrise. This could be what Mark meant, but there seems to be much more to it than that. Mark is wrestling with the meaning of the mystery of the grounds of new life in Christ. Mark is, I suggest, recording something of considerably greater import than a note of the time: we have not a chronological, but a theological account. For me, these verses of Mark provide one of the most moving passages in the New Testament. G.K. Chesterton catches up the image in his *The Everlasting Man*:

On the third day the friends of Christ coming at daybreak to the place found the grave empty and the stone rolled away. In varying ways they realised the new wonder, but even they hardly realised that the world had died in the night. What they were looking at was the first day of a new creation, with a new heaven and a new earth; and in the semblance of the gardener, God walked again in the garden, in the cool not of the evening but the dawn.[25]

'On the first day of the week': this is the first day of the new creation, the new order, for the old order is over. 'When the sun had risen': Mark, using a fragment of Roman myth, points to Christ as the *sol invictus*, the unconquered sun rising on his chariot in the heavens, hinting at the cosmic dimension of the exaltation of Christ: a theme also to the fore in the Pauline letters.

Even more curious is the end of this passage. This is hard to see in translation but the original *ephobounto gar* (for they were afraid) breaks off: the particle *gar* cannot in Greek conclude a

---

25. G.K. Chesterton, *The Everlasting Man*, Hodder & Stoughton, 1925, p. 244. I am grateful to Bernard Robinson, my former colleague at Ushaw, for alerting me to Chesterton's powerful passage.

sentence. It is as grammatically inappropriate and as tantalisingly open-ended as the definite article which concludes *Finnegans Wake*: we are led anew to the beginning of the story. It might of course be that the text was damaged at this point; verses 9–20 are certainly an addition to the original. Alternatively, there might be a hint here that there is no end to the gospel; that we, too, are now included in the story; though we may be frightened at the prospect, we have become witnesses in a dark world to the saving presence of Christ. We stand at the beginning of a new adventure.

If we can accept that John's gospel had knowledge of Luke's, we can see a similar thing happening here. The post-resurrection account of the disciples fishing expedition on the Sea of Galilee (Jn 21:1–9) is strangely reminiscent of Peter's first encounter with Jesus depicted in Luke 5:1–11: the fruitless labour of the night's trawling; the stranger's call to cast the nets again; the haul of fish; the call to conversion. The story begins once again, only the pace has quickened.

This gives us a clue to the nature of the post-resurrection narratives. Here the first disciples acknowledged an experiential awareness of their risen Lord and in their experience the Christian community recognises its own experience. A turning to scripture; the experience of forgiveness and healing; Eucharist; a commission to proclaim the good news; such experiences seem to provide the focus. We have very clear ecclesiological and liturgical themes here. The fragments which record the post-resurrection experiences are not merely fragments of memory, precious glimpses of the past to be preserved for their own sake and reflected on, to be passed on from one to another, but living – and life-giving – experiences for the community of Christians worshipping their Lord, and struggling to live out his call to give their lives in service to the world.

That first group of Christians, in the first light of a spring morning and then later in the warmth of early evening, were discovering Christ as a real and vibrant presence in their midst. And so do we. In their confusion they discovered him once more: not in a face but in the sound of a Word, the calling of a name. Mary, who knew him so well, just did not recognise him. She thought he was the gardener: 'Sir, if you have carried him away, tell me where you have laid him, and I will take him away.' Jesus said to her, 'Mary!' She turned and said to him, 'Rabbuni!', which means Teacher (Jn 20:15–16). It is the same for us: we do not meet him face-to-face as the first disciples did but find him in a word spoken: a word of healing; of forgiveness; a new name. Those two dejected ones on the way to Emmaus (a man and his wife, perhaps) had thought he had been the one to liberate Israel. They met a stranger who set their hearts on fire as he talked with them and explained the scriptures to them. They recognised him not in the glimpse of an eye around the supper table, but in a gesture: the gesture of breaking bread (Lk 24:13–32). It is the same for us: a gesture, eucharistic bread broken for a new world. The resurrection encounters are the stuff from which the church is fashioned; foundation narratives which give shape and energy to the lives of Christians.

CHAPTER FOUR

The Picture of Jesus in the Gospels

A Backwards look Forward

The resurrection does not belong to the closing pages of the gospels for it is the very reason the gospels came to be. The gospels are proclaimed with hindsight: they provide a backwards look forward. The resurrection is a discovery of new life in Christ. A group of dejected men and women, who had put their trust in Jesus and who scattered in fear when they witnessed the crucifixion, suddenly came to a newly confirmed experience of who Jesus is. This means we should hear the gospels in the light of the resurrection. The opening words of Mark's gospel set the scene: 'The beginning of the good news of Jesus Christ, the Son of God' (Mk 1:1). Jesus' shocking remark about disciples' taking up the cross, perhaps prompted by the remains of a gibbet stark on the skyline, takes on a profoundly different meaning after Jesus' own crucifixion (Mt 16:24). Abraham's comment to the rich man in the parable, 'If they do not listen to Moses and the prophets, neither will they be convinced even if someone rises from the dead' (Lk 16:19–31, see v. 31) reverberates on a very different note in the knowledge of Christ's own resurrection. Jesus himself comes to the centre of the picture:

> The parabler becomes the parable. Jesus announced the kingdom of God in parables, but the primitive church announced Jesus as the Christ, the Parable of God ... the Cross itself was not rejection but was itself the great Parable of God.[1]

As Crossan suggests the gospels are texts constantly shifting in meaning as we engage more deeply with them. This might be usefully illustrated by looking at the episode of the storm on the lake in Galilee.

---

1.   John Dominic Crossan, *The Dark Interval*, Illinois, 1973, pp. 124–5.

Mark 4:35–41	Luke 8:22–25	Matthew 8:23–27
On that day, when evening had come, he said to them, 'Let us go across to the other side.' And leaving the crowd behind, they took with them in the boat, just as he was. Other boats were with him.	One day he got into a boat with his disciples, and he said to them, 'Let us go across to the other side of the lake.' So they put out, and while they were sailing he fell asleep.	And when he got into the boat, his disciples followed him.
A great windstorm arose, and the waves beat into the boat, so that the boat was already being swamped. But he was in the stern, asleep on the cushion; and they woke him up and said to him,	A windstorm swept down on the lake, and the boat was filling with water, and they were in danger.	A windstorm arose on the sea, so great that the boat was being swamped by the waves; but he was asleep.
	They went to him and woke him up, shouting,	And they went and woke him up saying,
'Teacher, do you not care that we are perishing?'	'Master, Master, we are perishing!'	'Lord save us! We are perishing!' And he said to them, 'Why are you afraid, you of little faith?'
He woke up and rebuked the wind, and said to the sea, 'Peace! Be still!' Then the wind ceased, and there was a dead calm. He said to them, 'Why are you afraid? Have you still no faith?' And they were filled with great awe and said to one another, 'Who is this, that even the wind and sea obey him.	And he woke up and rebuked the wind and the raging waves; they ceased, and there was a calm. He said to them, 'Where is your faith?' They were afraid and amazed, and said to one another, 'Who then is this, that he commands even the winds and the water, and they obey him?'	Then he got up and rebuked the winds and the sea; and there was a great calm. (see above) They were amazed, saying, 'What sort of man is this, that even the winds and sea obey him?'

The earliest version of this account appears to be Mark's (col. 1). Mark has retained a lot of extraneous detail and the disciples treat Jesus roughly, almost rudely, as would make sense in such a frightening moment: 'Don't you care that the boat's going down?' One can almost sense the anger in their voices as they shake him roughly by the shoulder to get him to lend a hand with the bailing. Luke (col. 2) is rather more reverential; much of the detail is lost; 'Master' replaces Mark's 'Teacher', and the disciples seem a little more respectful. Matthew (col. 3) omits even more detail, presenting Christ as a majestic figure one might experience in an icon; now the disciples address Jesus in prayer: 'Lord save us! We are perishing!' Whoever the disciples understood Jesus to be at the time, there is no doubt that the author of the gospel understands him as Lord. One can imagine this as the prayer of a threatened and persecuted community: the barque of Peter is storm-tossed and the Lord of the church seems absent. They need the reassurance that the Lord of the storm is present and in control.

The gospel text is changing in focus as it is retold in the context of the needs and experiences of the contemporary community, not just remembering the text but entering into it and reliving it. The Jesus of John's gospel, which does not contain this incident, is more exalted yet. Jesus is depicted as being in control of the situation at all times, his human weakness virtually disappearing. Jesus' question to Philip before the feeding of the crowd, 'Where are we to buy bread for these people to eat?', was simply a test, 'for he himself knew what he was going to do' (Jn 6:5–6). Likewise in the garden of Gethsemane, the soldiers 'stepped back and fell to the ground' when Jesus identified himself (Jn 18:6). Yet this is the same Jesus we find in the other gospels.

The Real Humanity of Jesus the Christ

We tend to take the gospels for granted, overlooking just what strange documents they are. We might have had to be content with the proclamation of salvation, and perhaps with a collection of sayings of the Lord. But we have four gospels which give narrative shape to the life of Jesus. Such accounts provide a telling reminder that being human is constrained by time and by place. Remarks like 'but of course Jesus is God' or 'Jesus knows everything' need to be probed very carefully. A parent recently told me that her teenage son said to her that Jesus could never have cried, because he was God. How much damage to our understanding of the reality of Jesus has been done by the lines of the seemingly innocuous carol: 'The cattle are lowing, the baby awakes, but little Lord Jesus no crying he makes!' Of course he did. Jesus must have cried as lustily as any healthy baby for that is just what babies do when they are hungry, or scared, or teething.

The gospels stand as a constant challenge to any attempt to distract us from our search to respond to God's call to us in the midst of the messy, painful, sometimes joyful, sometimes tortuous, business which is the life of humans. Jesus could not speak English, nor would he have known the second law of thermodynamics. An abscess under a tooth would have been painful; he was not immune to the indignity of sickness and diarrhoea. That is what human life is like. It is the lot of humans to be caught in the warp and weft of history. It is here, too, that we find God; we cannot escape our embodied condition. The influential Jesuit theologian Karl Rahner invites us to reflect on three questions:

> Can Jesus tremble before the inconceivability of God?
> Can he, radically thrown back upon his own feeble
> creaturehood, adore God as the inconceivable?
> Can he go to meet a fate which is dark
> so far as he is concerned?[2]

At first sight it might be tempting to reply, 'Of course not; Jesus was God!' Rahner's answer is unexpected:

> Even though this 'ordinary consumer' [Christian] has himself
> all along been saying that Jesus is truly man, he will suddenly
> be brought up short and the 'yes' which he must pronounce in
> reply to this question will not come easily to his lips. And yet
> this 'yes' belongs to Catholic dogma right from the outset, and
> not merely to the findings of modern exegesis.[3]

We need to think hard about the implications of this.

---

2. Karl Rahner, *Theological Investigations*, vol. 11, DLT, p. 198.
3. Ibid.

Mary and Joseph taught Jesus the human activities that a growing boy of his time needed. He would have learnt to speak, to think, and to observe what was going on around, to learn the skills of Joseph's workshop. They would have taught him how to pray, to address God as his Father. He would have been taught how to listen to, and to interpret, the Hebrew scriptures; to recite the ancient prayers of his race. This is surely the theme underlying the story Luke tells of the finding in the Temple (Lk 2:41–52). Vatican II's *Constitution on the Church in the Modern World* puts it well in reminding us that Christ 'laboured with human hands, thought with a human mind, acted with a human will and loved with a human heart'.[4] And yet is a Christian's belief that, in the most felicitous words of Nicholas Lash, 'in every birth the flesh becomes word: a child cries. And the birth, or becoming, or historical production of the Christ is no exception. But in that child's cry, and in its consummation in the cry on the cross, there is uttered by man, in human flesh, the reality and mystery of God.'[5] Biological science offers us no insights into the divine nature of Jesus – nevertheless it is in and through that human being that we glimpse the mystery of God. In Jesus we find no God masquerading as human; no human being pointing the way to an unknown God; no hybrid creature, a mixture of the two, but Jesus Christ, Son of God, Word made flesh.

The world of first-century Palestine was very different to ours. Sometimes, looking back, certain events have a higher profile than they did for contemporaries. A superficial reading of the gospels might suggest that Jesus' great acts of healing are a clear pointer to his divine status. We need to be careful. The itinerant healer was a more familiar part of the rural scene than we might imagine. Geza Vermes, in his fascinating study of the Jewish context of Jesus, likens him to another famous charismatic healer, Honi the Circle-Drawer, who lived during the century before Jesus, and the Galilean, Hanina ben Dosa, a near contemporary of Jesus.[6] Healing, as at Lourdes today, is a powerful sign that God is present but is certainly not evidence that the one performing miracles is God. Jesus himself refused to use

---

4. *Gaudium et Spes*, § 22.
5. Nicholas Lash, *A Matter of Hope*, DLT, London, 1981, p. 144.
6. Geza Vermes, *Jesus the Jew*, Fontana, London, 1976, pp. 69–78.

miracles to prove his claim (Mk 8:11–12); he accepted without question that there were other Jewish exorcists amongst his contemporaries (Lk 11:21). As Bultmann comments:

> It is equally clear that Jesus did not, like the later apologists, think of miracles as a proof for the existence and rule of God; for he knew no doubt of God. Miracle indeed presupposes belief in God. Therefore Jesus put no special stress on his miracles, and at any rate is never greedy for miracles and does not, like other ancient and modern Messiahs, revel in his power of performing them.[7]

The Threshold of a New Age

What marks Jesus out from such figures is his preaching of the immanence of God's reign, the proclamation that we stand on the threshold of the new age. As he answers the disciples of John who come to ask, 'Are you he who is to come, or shall we look for another?':

> Go and tell John what you hear and see: the blind receive their sight and the lame walk, lepers are cleansed and the deaf hear, and the dead are raised up, and the poor have the good news preached to them. And blessed is he who takes no offence at me. (Mt 11:3–6 / / Lk 7:19–23. See Is 29:18–19; 35:5–6; 61:1)

The miracles are not only signs of God's healing compassion, but are linked intimately to the proclamation of God's reign.

At the heart of Jesus' teaching lie the parables, which in various ways alert his hearers to the in-breaking of God's reign. These are far more than mere illustrations of his teaching: they seek to draw the listener in, to help her experience a foretaste of God's reign. We need discernment here. Originally told to awaken his Jewish contemporaries to the immanent arrival of God's reign, with the emergence of the gospels the parables have been reworked as proclamation to the community of disciples. This changes their focus.

In the context of Christian preaching, the parable of the Sower becomes a story about the reception of Jesus' message (Mk 4:3–20). The allegorising explanation (vv. 10–20) is generally accepted as an example of early church teaching: the focus is

---

7. Rudolf Bultmann, *Jesus and the Word*, Fontana, London, 1958, p. 124. 10. 10. Schillebeeckx, *Jesus*, p. 542.

no longer the seed, but the areas in which it is sown. The twenty-first-century mind, used to Western farming methods, can easily miss the passionate love determining the story. In the poor, arid soil of Palestine, seed was sown first, and only then ploughed in. There were no proper fields, just land around the village, some parts better than others, crisscrossed with paths, and occasionally with the underlying rock coming to the surface, or at least stones. The seed was scattered prodigally, and ploughing came second, so that even the tiniest pockets of good soil might be made fruitful. The resultant crop does not contrast rich pastures of fruitful wheat with fruitless soil, but rejoices that even in the tiniest pockets of our stony hearts God's love finds an echo. In parable after parable, we are led to experience God's passionate love for wayward humanity: the shepherd profligately abandoning his flock to search out the lost (Mt 18:12–14); the elderly patriarch making himself look silly running out to meet his spendthrift son (Lk 15:11–23).

The Heart of Jesus' Experience
It is often suggested that the parables reveal Jesus as teacher *par excellence*, engaging with, and drawing out, his audience. I think we can go further. The parables also suggest that he was so caught up in the mystery of God that wherever he looked he saw the love of his Father. In the shepherd caring for his flock (Mt 18:10–14//Lk 15:3–7); the woman kneading dough (Mt 13:33//Lk 13:20–21); the vineyard owner hiring labourers (Mt 20:1–16), the merchant seeking fine pearls (Mt 13:44–46), Jesus could not help but discover the mystery of God's very depths which was the heart of his own experience.

There a few words of Aramaic preserved in the Greek of the New Testament texts. They are nearly always found on the lips of Jesus: *amēn* (Mk 3:28; 9:41); *talitha cum* ('Little girl, get up' Mk 5:41); *ephphatha* ('Be opened' Mk 7:34). One might wonder why such words have been preserved. It is a good guess that they are memories of the actual words of Jesus saved like flies in amber. Like the Jewish community we regularly use *amen* to affirm prayer: 'So be it', 'I agree'. The use of the word *amen* to introduce a saying is unique to the New Testament and is found only on the lips of Jesus (with the possible exception of Mk 16:20), 30 times in Matthew, 13 times in Mark, 6 times in Luke, and in John, always in a double form, 25 times. It is sometimes missed in English translation: see for example, 'For truly (*amēn*) I tell you until heaven and earth pass away, not one letter, not one stroke of a letter, will pass from the law until all is accomplished' (Mt 5:18). There can be no doubt that here we have a genuine idiom of Jesus and that Jesus uses the expression to affirm God's authentication of his words:

> Jesus identifies himself entirely with his words, that in the identification with these words he surrenders himself to the reality of God, and that he lets his existence be grounded in God's making these words true and real. That means, he is so certain of these words that he stakes his whole self on that certainty.[8]

It could well be for this reason that, in the Book of Revelation, 'Amen' becomes personified as a title for the Lord himself (Rev 3:14: 'The words of the Amen, the faithful and true witness, the origin of God's creation') and, as Christ was God's Yes to us, those who are incorporated in him, are caught up in the great hymn of praise which is 'the "Amen" to the glory of God' (2 Cor 1:17–22).

Another of these words, *abba* (father) occurs three times in the New Testament: once as Jesus addressed his heavenly Father during the agony in Gethsemane (Mk 14:36), and twice in the letters of St Paul (Rom 8:15; Gal 4:6). Here in prayer we are surely drawn into the intimacy of Jesus' own relationship with his Father. There are other echoes of similar usage: while the Matthean version of the Lord's Prayer (Mt 6:9–15) seems to have been assimilated to the patterns of prayer found in the synagogue, Luke's rather simpler version (Lk 11:2–4) could reflect another example of this intimate usage.

Much has been written about the word, *abba*. Some have suggested it is more akin to the English 'Daddy', the address of a child to a loving, protecting father. This is perhaps going a little far, but while not absolutely unprecedented in Jewish literature of the time, it does suggest Jesus lived out an intimacy with God that was rather different from his contemporaries, and that he taught his followers to do likewise.[9] What

---

8. Gerhard Ebeling, *Word and Faith*, SCM London, 1984, p. 237.
9. Joachim Jeremias, *The Prayers of Jesus*, SCM, London, 1967, pp. 11–65; James Barr, 'Abba isn't Daddy', *Journal of Theological Studies*, 39, 1988, pp. 28–47; Edward Schillebeeckx, *Jesus*, pp. 256–71.

Schillebeeckx calls Jesus' 'Abba experience' becomes a symbol for our understanding of the grounding of Jesus' life in the mystery of God.[10]

As we have seen, some Jewish scholars such as Vermes claim that we can make sense of Jesus as a Jewish rabbi, or itinerant healer, by placing him firmly in the context of first-century Palestine. This position is challenged by another Jewish scholar, Jacob Neusner, in his important meditation on the Sermon on the Mount, *A Rabbi talks with Jesus*.[11] Neusner argues that Jesus stands in sharp contradiction to the Judaism of his time and that the Torah, the Law of the Old Testament, stands in judgement on Jesus' teaching on a number of occasions.[12] In a series of passages about the law found in the second half of Matthew 5, Jesus contrasts the teaching of the past with his own demands on his disciples: 'You have it that it was said to those of ancient times ... But I say to you ...' (Mt 5:21–26; 27–30; 31–32; 33–42; 43–48). Matthew records that, in words found also in Mark's gospel, the people were astonished because 'he taught them as one having authority, and not as their scribes' (Mt 6:26//Mk 1:21). He speaks, as the Greek has it, *exousia*, out of his very being. This personal authority, echoed in the frequent 'I myself (*ego eimi*) ...' of John's gospel, is something no Jewish rabbi could claim, setting his own interpretation against the revealed Torah of God.[13] Although Neusner does not make the point, the same can be said for Jesus' identification with the Temple in one of the most well attested verses in the gospels: 'Destroy this Temple and in three days I will raise it up' (Jn 2:19; see also Mt 26:61; Mk 14:58). John makes clear he was speaking of the temple of his body (Jn 2:21).

Neusner's examination of Jesus' handling of the commandments about the holiness of the Sabbath rest, and honouring one's father and mother, only serve to intensify the point (Mt 12:1–8, 46–50): 'Jesus calls into question the primacy of the family in the priority of my responsibilities, the centrality of the

---

10. Schillebeeckx, *Jesus*, p. 542.
11. McGill–Queen's University Press, Montreal, Kingston, London and Ithaca, 2000. This is a book Benedict XVI writes enthusiastically about in his *Jesus of Nazareth*, Bloomsbury, 2007.
12. Op. cit., p. 23.
13. Op. cit., pp. 46–7.

family in the social order.'[14] Jesus makes personal demands on his followers, so much so that Neusner can only conclude that 'only God can demand of me what Jesus is asking'.[15] The weary traveller, returning from the cities of the diaspora, was encouraged to shake off the dust of pagan territories before stepping on the holy land. Jesus significantly changes the metaphor. It is no longer the holy land that is important but wherever there is a welcome for the message of the gospel:

> And if any one will not welcome you or listen to your words, shake of the dust from your feet as you leave that house or town. (Mt 10:14//Mk 6:11//Lk 9:5, 10:11)

There is a profound rediscovery of the sacred taking place here. Perhaps better, a profound rediscovery of the secular for, as Neusner comments:

> Sanctification categorically requires the designation of what is holy against what is not holy. To sanctify is to set apart. No sanctification can encompass everyone or leave room for someone in particular to be holy ... The kingdom of Heaven, coming soon, has nothing to do with this; what is at issue is gaining access into God's kingdom.[16]

This is precisely Jesus' point. There are no longer any sacred places, for the whole world is holy: the body of Jesus replaces the Temple; commitment to him is the keeping of the Torah. Every space is holy which affords a welcome to those who preach the good news. The disciple cannot define herself over against another. Jesus eats and consorts with those beyond the safe haven of the community: the lepers, the prostitutes, the tax collectors. And as he did, so must we, as we live out the pattern of his life.

The Challenge of Jesus to the Prevailing System

Although Jesus had not blasphemed in the technical sense by pronouncing the name YHWH, his teaching represented a challenge to the heart of Judaism. The Jewish leaders were in open conflict with Jesus on the matter of contemporary attitudes to

---

14. Op. cit., p. 58.
15. Op. cit., p. 68.
16. Op. cit., p. 123.

the Law, Sabbath observance, the sanctity of the Temple. In teaching, highlighted by such provocative parables as that of the Wicked Tenants (Mk 12:1–12, and parallels), by his very presence among them and through all that he stood for, Jesus was demanding from the Jews a radical change of attitude towards the things they considered central.

The Sanhedrin, although consisting of individuals who held significantly different views regarding aspects of Judaism, could agree on one point: that Jesus must be dealt with. Unable to reconcile the teaching of Jesus with their belief, they were convinced that he was a dangerous person who was perverting the minds of the people and who must be totally discredited. An illegal lynching, or back street stoning, though possible (as just a short time later the stoning of Stephen bears ample witness), would not be sufficient to discredit Jesus and might even turn him into something of a martyr for upholding the cause of the common people with whom he was identified. The New Testament scholar Joachim Jeremias points out that 'it is not inconceivable that Mt 23:37 par. Luke 13:34 hints that for a time Jesus considered the possibility of stoning, the penalty of which he had repeatedly incurred.'[17]

The Sanhedrin needed to seek a motive at law by which they could do away with Jesus. From the official Jewish point of view the abhorrent Roman punishment of crucifixion would be particularly appropriate: it would placate the Roman administration, showing that the recalcitrant and suspect Jews were prepared (quite unusually) to have someone put to death for treason against the Roman occupying forces. More significantly, for the Jews themselves the very act of crucifixion was a sign of God's curse (Deut 21:23): such a scriptural background might well underlie the inconclusive debates of the Sanhedrin and suggest a motive for this particular choice of death as they rushed Jesus to crucifixion. There are possible allusions to this text in the sermon passages recorded in Acts (See Acts 5:30; 10:39; 13:29). Crucifixion would demonstrate beyond doubt that Jesus was a 'false teacher'. This is the argument that Paul turns on its head in his letter to the Galatians:

---

17. Joachim Jeremias, *New Testament Theology*, vol. 1, SCM, London, 1976, p. 284.

Christ redeemed us from the curse of the law by becoming a curse for us – for it is written, 'Cursed is everyone who hangs on a tree' – in order that in Christ Jesus the blessing of Abraham might come to the Gentiles (Gal 3:13–14).

The Coherence of the New Testament witness to the One Lord and Christ

Adolph von Harnack argued that the simple gospel message had been corrupted by its association with the complexities of Hellenic philosophical categories. He attempted to draw a clear division between the pastoral simplicities of the gospels and the theological contortions of Saint Paul. In his influential *What is Christianity?*,[18] von Harnack claimed that dogma was divisive and suggested that we should focus on the person of Jesus who preached of a common heavenly Father and a message of love uncontaminated by doctrine. A comparison of the material we find in the gospels with the earlier interpretation of Jesus Christ in the Pauline writings and other fragments of literature preserved from the earliest communities allows us to conclude that we cannot make such a division between Paul and the gospels. There is a dramatic similarity of approach. C.F.D. Moule spells this out clearly:

> At no point in the New Testament, so far as I can see, is there any suggestion that Christian experience meant no more than that it was the teaching and example of a figure of the past which now enabled Christians to approach God with a new understanding and confidence ... On the contrary they believed that it was because the same Jesus was alive and was himself in some way in touch with them there and then that the new relationship and the new freedom were made possible ... The transcendent, divine person of present experience was continuous and identical with the historical figure of the past.[19]

It is just not true, as scholars such as Adolph von Harnack once argued, that Paul converted stories of a Jewish rabbi into the

---

18. Adolph von Harnack, *Das Wesen des Christentums*, 1900; Eng. trs. *What is Christianity?*, 1901.
19. C.F.D. Moule, *The Phenomenon of the New Testament*, SCM, London, 1967, pp. 96–106; passage sited from p. 99.

Christ of the church and that, as a result, it is Paul who ought to be regarded as the inventor of Christianity.

Already by the end of the 30s of the Common Era, the group of Jesus followers were being identified as 'Christians' in the cosmopolitan town of Antioch (Acts 11:26). The German New Testament scholar, Martin Hengel, comments:

> In the short space of less than twenty years the crucified Galilean Jew, Jesus of Nazareth, was elevated by his followers to a dignity which left every possible form of pagan-polytheistic apotheosis far behind ... Pre-existence, Mediator of Creation and the revelation of his identity with the One God: this exceeds the possibilities of deification in a polytheistic pantheon; here we have a new ... category before us that must be explained from first Christian experience, or as the case may be, from its Jewish background.[20]

The evidence suggests that an inevitable and appropriate interpretation that Jesus is Lord can be judged not to be untrue to the picture of Jesus as it emerged in the gospels.

---

20. Martin Hengel, *Studies in Early Christology*, T&T Clark, Edinburgh, 1995, pp. 383–4.

CHAPTER FIVE

A New Vocabulary

Differing Approaches but One Christ
Many scholars argue that we should be slow to relinquish the pluralism of the differing New Testament approaches to christology and that these might be fruitfully regarded as possible starting points for new and exciting christologies, better attuned to the needs of Asian and African cultures, as well as our own postmodern society, that find terminology inherited from the Graeco–Roman world alien and unhelpful. This variety of approaches helps also in establishing ways in which Christians might engage in dialogue with the other great faiths. The early church can be regarded as a melting pot of ideas which might offer important clues to new formulations of our belief: this is an exciting moment for students of christology. Scholars note that functional language is more reflective of the Semitic styles of thought which formed the earliest expression of christology. Some suggest that we are right to identify a progression in the New Testament from the earliest christologies towards the more fully incarnational, ontological christology of John which becomes increasingly normative for the faith of the church.

In the first centuries after the shaping of the New Testament texts, the church was forced to clarify its thinking about Jesus. Disagreements and heresies sprang up. The latter is best defined simply as a truth isolated and pushed to extremes, breaking the coherence of tradition and overemphasising a part of it, now out of proportion with the rest. Some insisted on the divinity of Jesus to the exclusion of his humanity, others stressed that he was human through and through, merely pointing to a distant and mysterious God like the prophets of old; still others tried to suggest he was a hybrid being, partly human, partly divine. The task of the praying community of the church was to maintain and clarify its belief that Jesus is truly human, truly divine. To do this, a new vocabulary had gradually to be coined.

The first task was to do justice to the New Testament insight that in Jesus God is at work. But the Jewish community and the Christians who followed in their footsteps were passionate monotheists (believers in one God) and they needed to reconcile their monotheism with their experience of Jesus. It is important to emphasise the fact that all the writings of the following centuries are nothing more than this. The work of the Fathers, the studies of great theologians such as Thomas Aquinas in the Middle Ages, and Rahner and Barth in modern times, are, for all their fashioning of technical terms, simply, and no more than, a series of attempts to do justice to the narrative of the New Testament. The doctrine of the Trinity is simply a way of articulating Paul's profound summary of revelation: 'God was in Christ reconciling the world to himself' (2 Cor 5:19). As Bernard Lonergan has said in his *The Way to Nicea*, when we come to talk of

> the Nicene concept of consubstantiality [we do not] go beyond the dogmatic realism that is contained implicitly in the word of God. For it means no more than this, that what is said of the Father is to be said also of the Son, except that the Son is Son and not the Father.[1]

Such terms, tempered in the fires of fierce discussion, are simply guidelines laid down to assist us in the interpretation of the scriptures.

The initial step, as we have seen, was already spelt out in the work of Paul, and in the great hymn found in the prologue to John's gospel (Jn 1:1–18). This rooted the experience of Christ deep in the wisdom tradition of the Hebrew scriptures but also linked him with the tradition of Greek thought which depicted the Word as the principle of rationality embedded in the universe. This was a theme developed by the earliest Christian thinkers: Ignatius, Justin Martyr, Athenagoras, Irenaeus, and others.

Other views sprang up. Some, perhaps familiar with the Greek stories of the gods appearing in human form, stressed Jesus' divinity to the exclusion of his humanity. This is what is called docetism: God merely appearing/seeming to be human but not really so. The opposite tendency tried to preserve God's

---

1. Bernard Lonergan, *The Way to Nicea*, DLT, London, 1976, p. 130.

transcendence by treating Jesus as merely a prophet, the embod-
iment of the Logos as less than God: a being external to God,
merely pointing to a distant majesty.

Nicaea (325) and its aftermath

The question came to a head with the work of Arius (c.250–336),
a brilliant Alexandrian priest, well versed in scripture. Arius
took Prov 8:22–31 (see above, pp. 23–4) as a central text, insisting
that to take the biblical account seriously it must be argued that
Wisdom, God's agent of creation, must itself be created, a product of God's will, not an expression of God's being, a sign of
God's distance from the created universe. Here is not a 'second
God' over against the Father, still less a sort of attenuation of
God's reality for it was clear to Arius, being well versed in
Greek thought, that a divine being could not suffer. Though
originating as an extreme example of divine transcendence, his
thought ends up by asserting an insurmountable division between God and a created intermediary. It can be sketched out in
the accompanying diagram. The central line represents orthodoxy while the extremes (those to the left overemphasising divinity, to the right, overemphasising humanity) shade off into
heresy. Diagrammatically, Arius represents something of a
problem because first and foremost he wished to preserve a
biblical understanding of God's transcendence and ends by
insisting that God's agent in creation is himself merely another
created being, subject to change and alteration.

Athanasius (296–373) countered such thinking by establishing a vital principle: a true account of Christ must be founded on
soteriology (the doctrine of salvation). If being attentive to the
nuances of scripture is the first criterion of christology, being
attentive to the need to proclaim salvation is the second. We
must ask not simply who Christ is, but why Christ; what is
Christ doing? Only God can save, and because Christ not only
proclaims our salvation but brings it about, Christ must therefore be divine. God does not deal with creation by hiding
behind an intermediary, but in Christ, we see God as God is, a
merciful and loving God. In keeping with this, Athanasius
prefers to refer to Christ as Son, rather than as Logos. This was
the conclusion of the first council of the church held at Nicaea

(325), which in its attempt to be true to the biblical picture of Christ introduced a non-biblical word to the heart of the Church's faith: *homoousios* (of the same substance as/of the same being as). Using this word was the only way the church Fathers could counteract Arius who had already refused to accept the term. Many bishops, however, were very uneasy: the word had a rather dubious background in various heresies and many would have preferred to confine themselves to biblical terminology. Concerns about the use of such a word led to a backlash in the years immediately following the council of Nicaea.

The period from Nicaea to Constantinople was described by St Basil as a naval battle in thick darkness.[2] Many eastern bishops, trained in the tradition of the great Origen, feared that Nicaea was asking them to disown Origen as the price of excluding Arius. Some bishops argued that *homoousios* conceded too much, and that it would be better to say that Christ was *homoiousios* (of similar substance/of similar being) to the Father. The Eastern Fathers suspected the West of denying the permanent reality of the Three Persons in God by teaching that God was One Being merely taking on a different form in relation to different periods of history (modalism, a theory associated with the rather shadowy early third-century figure, Sabellius). Still more crudely they were accused of holding that the 'one substance' which was God was some sort of spirituous matter, somehow divided up into bits to express the persons. *Homoiousios* was thus offered as an antidote to the modalism, which they feared that the West was imposing on them by an uncritical acceptance of *homoousios*. These eastern bishops, in turn, wanted to reassert Origen's emphasis on the Three Persons by rescuing it from the constraints imposed by his tendency to subordinate the Son and Spirit to the Father (subordinationism).

---

2. 'It may be compared, I think, to some naval battle which has arisen out of time old quarrels, and is fought by men who cherish a deadly hate against one another, of long experience in naval warfare, and eager for the fight … Fancy, if you like, the ships driven to and fro by a raging tempest, while thick darkness falls from the clouds and blackens all the scene, so that watchwords are indistinguishable in the confusion, and all distinction between friend and foe is lost' (Basil, *On the Holy Spirit*, p. 76). The image was taken up and adapted by Newman for the conclusion of his sermon, 'Faith and Reason, contrasted as Habits of Mind' (*University Sermons*, SPCK, London, 1970, p. 201); it returns in the final lines of Matthew Arnold's *Dover Beach*.

Towards the Expression of Orthodoxy I

Jesus Christ

truly divine	*truly human*
Docetism (God dressed up as man: Greek emphasis on transcendence of God)	*Adoptionism* (Jesus a prophet who speaks for God: Hebrew emphasis on transcendence of God)

LOGOS
(Plato/Stoic) Word as creative agency which mediates between God and Creation – present in universe but made visible in Jesus (Jn 1:14)

Modalism e.g. Sabellius (early third century) – for Tertullian this picture a *'turncoat god'*

Arianism (Arius c.250–336) Divine present in Jesus but still less than God (made not begotten)

Athanasius
(c.296–373)

NICAEA (325)
necessary intrusion of Greek term to preserve Biblical insight (*homoousios*)

Cappadocian Settlement

CONSTANTINOPLE (381)

For the young Thomas Carlyle this seemed merely a silly dispute about a diphthong (the difference between the pronunciation of the Greek vowels *o* and *oi*), but a lot more is at stake, as Carlyle later realised.[3] Do we indeed experience who God truly is in the life, death and resurrection of Jesus, or could God be hiding behind a mask so that God in God's very self might remain a strange, alien reality? The issue is rather more important. In Christ, God reveals God as God truly is. There is no deception here, no differentiation between how God encounters the world and how God is in the unfathomable depths of God's very being. The life, death and resurrection of Christ spell out the Father's redeeming love for humanity: 'God so loved the world that he gave his only Son, so that everyone who believes in him may not perish but may have eternal life' (Jn 3:16).

The Council of Constantinople (381)

This issue was settled when the Council Fathers at Constantinople (381) reaffirmed the Creed of Nicaea. The Creed we affirm in our liturgy is the Creed of both Councils: the Niceno–Constantinopolitan Creed, merely Nicene for short. The three Cappadocian Fathers (Gregory of Nyssa, Basil, his brother, and Gregory of Nazianzus) made the necessary breakthrough by insisting that to talk of the unity of God is to talk in personal categories. *Hypostasis* (a concept akin to *being*) is now to be understood as a way of expressing the Persons of the Trinity. Relation is understood as not only a relationship between already existing Persons but as actually constituting the Persons (the Father can only be understood as the *Father of* the Son; the Son, *Son of* the Father; the Spirit, *the Spirit of* the Father). This was something not quite picked up by Augustine and the later Western tradition which teaches an understanding of the Trinity which appears more static, lacking the dynamism of the Cappadocian view.

---

3. 'In speaking of Gibbon's work to me he made one remark which is worth recording. In earlier years he had spoken contemptuously of the Athanasian controversy, of the Christian world torn in pieces over a diphthong, and he would ring the changes in broad Annandale on the Homoousion and the Homoiousion. He told me now that he perceived Christianity itself to have been at stake. If the Arians had won, it would have dwindled away into a legend' (J.A. Froude, *Thomas Carlyle: A Life in London*, 1884, vol. 2, p. 486).

A comparison of the Creeds of these two councils shows how Nicaea adopted an earlier baptismal Creed, adapting it to stand solidly against Arius, both in its insistence on the use of the word *homoousios* and by adding a little collection of sayings associated with Arius and denying them forcefully. Nicaea adopted the metaphor of begetting, rather than making/creating, to underline the intimate relationship between Father and Son: the Son is not created, or made, nor, of course, biologically begotten, but his person is the full expression of the mystery of God. Constantinople smooths out the phraseology of the Creed, adding phrases relating to the Virgin Birth and Christ's death under the procuratorship of Pontius Pilate, as well as considerably extending the third article of the Creed concerning the Holy Spirit and the mystery of the church.

The Creed of Nicaea (325)	*The Creed of Constantinople (381)*
We believe in one God the Father Almighty, maker of all things visible and invisible.	We believe in one God the Father almighty, maker of heaven and earth, maker of all things visible and invisible.
And in one Lord Jesus Christ, the Son of God, only-begotten, born of the Father, that is from the substance (*ousia*) of the Father, God from God, light from light, true God from true God, born not made, of one substance with (*homoousios*) the Father, through whom all things were made, both in heaven and on earth; for us humans and for our salvation he came down and became flesh, became human,	And in one Lord Jesus Christ, the only begotten Son of God, born of the Father before all ages, light from light, true God from true God, born not made, of one substance with (*homoousios*) the Father, through whom all things were made. For us humans and for our salvation he came down from the heavens and became flesh of the Holy Spirit and of the virgin Mary, became human and was crucified on our behalf under Pontius Pilate; he suffered and was buried
suffered and rose on the third day, went up into the heavens,	and rose up on the third day, in accordance with the scriptures; and he went up into the heavens

is coming	and is seated at the right hand of the Father; he shall come again in glory
to judge the living and the dead.	to judge the living and the dead; of whose kingdom there will be no end.
And in the Holy Spirit.	And in the Spirit, the Holy, the Lord, and the Life-giving, who proceeds from the Father, co-worshipped and co-glorified with the Father and the Son, the one who spoke through the prophets; in one, holy, catholic and apostolic church; we confess one baptism for the forgiveness of sins and we look forward to the resurrection of the dead and the life of the world to come. Amen.
But to those who say 'there was when he was not', and 'before he was born, he was not', and 'that he was made out of nothing' or out of some other substance or being, or that the Son of God is subject to change and alteration, such the Catholic Church declares anathema.	

Nicaea and Constantinople established the relationship between Father, Son and Holy Spirit. The next task to come to the fore was to seek to mark out the relationship between divine and human in Jesus Christ.

The Christological Settlement
The diagram below shows the move towards orthodoxy in the period up to the Third Council of Constantinople in 681. There were two main influential schools of thought in the East: the Alexandrian tradition, based in the cosmopolitan city of the Nile delta, and the school of Antioch in Northern Syria. The former, represented by figures such as Athanasius, Appolinarius and Cyril took its cue from John 1:14 ('and the Word became flesh'), and developed a Word-flesh (*logos-sarx*), incarnational

christology which focused on the unity of the person of the Word/Son who took on human flesh. By assuming human flesh the Word/Son brought salvation to a transfigured, deified humanity. Jesus' humanity tended to be understood as a passive instrument of the Word. Athanasius and Appolinarius do not appreciate the need to claim that Jesus had a human soul and, in failing to work out a fully coherent understanding of what it means to be a human being, this tradition failed to offer an acceptable account of Jesus' full humanity. This party took as their battle cry the phrase 'the one nature (*monos physis*) of God the word made flesh', a phrase attributed to the great Athanasius, but in fact coined by his heretical follower, Appolinarius. As a result, the group became known as monophysites (the one nature people). For a lesser thinker such as Eutyches, this position drifted into regarding Christ as a sort of hybrid, a mixture of human and divine.

The Antiochene tradition, represented by Theodore of Mopsuestia and Nestorius, in contrast, sought to give full justice to Jesus' humanity in the work of salvation. Starting from a Word–Human being (*logos-anthrōpos*) christology, this school of thought stressed the dual nature of Christ, at times presenting him almost as a committee of two working in harmony, divine and human. By emphasising the distinction between the divinity and humanity in Jesus Christ these theologians failed to find a way of doing justice to the unity which the Alexandrian tradition realised must lie at the heart of the doctrine. As Roger Haight suggests, the problem lay in the preconceptions they received from the tradition to which they belonged:

> with the individualisation of the Logos, there are 'two', Logos as an individual and the individual human being Jesus, out of which one cannot make 'one' without compromising one or the other. What one finds in this christology is not dialectical thinking but an impossible conceptual dilemma.[4]

A Council at Ephesus (431) was hurriedly opened, Cyril beginning deliberations so that he could impose his views on the Council before the arrival of Nestorius and the eastern bishops. The latter, under the leadership of John of Antioch, on their

---

4. Roger Haight, *Jesus Symbol of God*, Orbis Books, Maryknoll, 1999, p. 270.

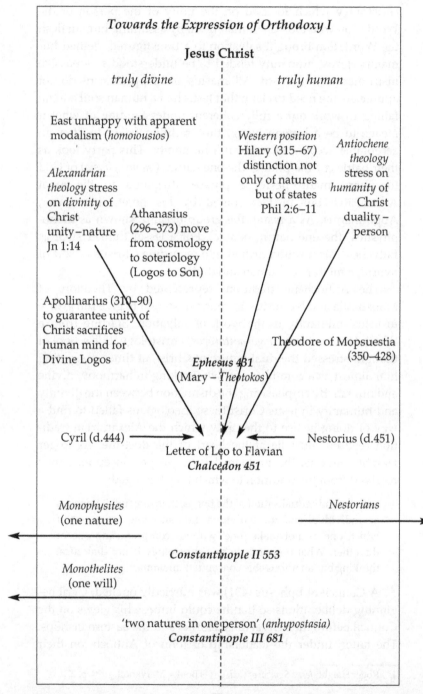

Towards the Expression of Orthodoxy I

Jesus Christ

truly divine | *truly human*

East unhappy with apparent modalism (*homoiousios*)

Alexandrian theology stress on *divinity* of Christ unity–nature Jn 1:14

Athanasius (296–373) move from cosmology to soteriology (Logos to Son)

Western position Hilary (315–67) distinction not only of natures but of states Phil 2:6–11

Antiochene theology stress on *humanity* of Christ duality – person

Apollinarius (310–90) to guarantee unity of Christ sacrifices human mind for Divine Logos

Ephesus 431 (Mary – *Theotokos*)

Theodore of Mopsuestia (350–428)

Cyril (d.444) → Letter of Leo to Flavian *Chalcedon 451* ← Nestorius (d.451)

Monophysites (one nature)

Nestorians

Constantinople II 553

Monothelites (one will)

'two natures in one person' (*anhypostasia*)
Constantinople III 681

arrival at Ephesus established an opposing council. With the eventual appearance of the legates from Rome, the Council continued its work, endorsing Cyril's position and condemning Nestorius and John of Antioch. Ephesus affirmed Mary's full role as *theotokos* (Mother of God), not *Christotokos* (Christ bearer), as Nestorius at first preferred. Nestorius was eventually exiled to the desert (436) for preaching 'two Sons', a charge he always denied. Cyril eventually came to accept John's profession of faith and agreed to a compromise statement, the Formula of Reunion (433) largely composed by John.

The Contribution of the West and Tome of Leo
Although moving more closely together than they realised, these two schools of thought faced an impasse, each emphasising the errors of the opposing school without appreciating what they held in common. A solution was needed which could draw together the strengths of both traditions into a common formula. This came from the West. Represented by such figures as Hilary of Poitiers and Leo the Great, these thinkers may have lacked the subtlety of Greek thought but they remained clear on the issues at stake, like the straight Roman road travelling somewhat roughshod from A to B and failing to be attentive to the meandering complexity of issues through which it journeyed. Hilary emphasised not just the static conjunction of the two natures but set these within a dynamic of history, the pattern being set by Phil 2:5–11:

- the Son is God before the incarnation;
- the Son is both God and human during the period of the incarnation;
- the Son is fully human and fully divine after exaltation to the right hand of the Father.

In discussing the incarnation Hilary invoked the Pauline imagery of *kenōsis* (Phil 2:7: *self-emptying*: the renunciation of the form of God by taking on the form of a servant: a shrouding, not obliteration, of divinity during Jesus' life on earth).

With Nestorius still in exile, the chief danger was from the hard-line supporters of Cyril, who had died in 444, such as Eutyches and Dioscorus. They reacted against the Formula of

Reunion in a strongly monophysite direction. Flavian, Patriarch of Constantinople, censured Eutyches, the 'muddle-headed archimandrite',[5] who argued that Christ, though two natures before the union was 'one nature after the union' and that this one nature was divine and not 'of one substance with us': Christ was God *appearing* in human form. Eutyches, with the support of Cyril's successor in Alexandria, Dioscorus, was vindicated by a synod held in Ephesus (449, nicknamed the *latrocinium*, 'robber synod' by Pope Leo) and Flavian was condemned, soon dying as a result of ill-treatment.

Flavian's earlier appeal to Rome won the support of Leo, who made his position clear in his letter to Flavian (the tome of Leo), in which he developed the thoughts of Hilary in a series of stark and dramatic contrasts:

> Without detriment therefore to the properties of either nature and substance which then came together in one person, majesty took on humility, strength weakness, eternity mortality: and for the paying off of the debt belonging to our condition inviolable nature was united with passible nature, so that, as suited the needs of our case, one and the same Mediator between God and men, the Man Christ Jesus, could both die with the one and not die with the other ... He took the form of a slave without stain of sin, increasing the human and not diminishing the divine: because that emptying (*kenōsis*) of himself whereby the Invisible made himself visible and, Creator and Lord of all things though he be, wished to be a mortal, was the bending down of pity, not the failing of power.[6]

Like Irenaeus and Athanasius before them, Hilary and Leo insisted that human salvation and wholeness is dependent not simply on the work of Christ but on his person: 'we were raised because He was lowered; shame to Him was glory to us. He being God made flesh his residence, and we in turn are lifted up anew from flesh to God.'[7]

---

5. J.N.D. Kelly, *Early Christian Doctrines*, Adam & Charles Black, London, 1965, p. 331.
6. Leo the Great, *Letter* 28, in P. Schaff and Henry Wace, *Letters and Sermons of Leo the Great, The Nicene & Post-Nicene Fathers of the Christian Church*, Second Series, T&T Clark, Edinburgh, 1997, vol. 12, p. 40.
7. Hilary of Poitiers, *On the Trinity*, in E.W. Watson and L. Pullan, *St Hilary of Poitiers: Select Works, The Nicene & Post-Nicene Fathers of the Christian Church*, Second Series, T&T Clark, Edinburgh, 1997, p. 59.

The empress Pulcheria, the power behind the throne, supported Flavian and Leo, and a new council was called to meet in Chalcedon, across the Bosphorus from Constantinople, to deal with the monophysite threat. While the tone of the resultant Creed appears to reflect an Alexandrian emphasis on the unity of the person, it differs significantly from Cyril's approach. Cyril regularly emphasised the Word as subject in the tradition he inherited form Appolinarius. Chalcedon emphasises the concrete reality of the Lord Jesus Christ as subject: we find God in the life and ministry of the person we encounter in the gospels. The terminology of the Council relied heavily on the phraseology of Leo's letter, which many bishops thought veered too close to the Antiochenes. Chalcedon produced a christological definition, safeguarding the Antiochene insistence on distinction of natures, but in terms drawn from Cyril's writings. This definition reversed the main terms of the debate, using the Alexandrian insistence on nature (*physis*) as now expressing the duality of divine and human in Christ, and the Antiochene person (*prosōpon*) as guarantee of the unity of the two natures. The proposed wording 'out of (or from) two natures' was changed in the fifth session to satisfy the West and other bishops of the Antiochene party. It incorporated Leo's insistence that Christ is known 'in two natures'[8] in clear opposition to the more extreme disciples of Cyril.

---

8. Leo the Great, ibid. For a useful commentary see, Anthony Baxter, 'Chalcedon, and the Subject in Christ', *Downside Review*, vol. 107, no. 366, January 1989, pp. 1–21.

Defining Nature and Person

divine	*human*
nature	*nature*

hypostasis
person

the one and the same Son and Only-begotten,
the divine Logos, the Lord Jesus Christ

Nature (Greek: *physis*; Latin: *natura*) simply and nothing more than the answer to the question '*What* is this?' 'This is a human being'; 'This is a mouse.' There are, of course, no such things as 'natures' floating about; there are only particular humans, or particular mice, with all their quirks and singularities.

Person (Greek: *prosōpon*; plural *prosōpa*; Latin: *persona*, plural *personae*) is simply and nothing more than the answer to the question, '*Who* is this?' 'This is John'; or 'This is Mary.' The word originated in the language of the Greek theatre, but then took on further meanings:

  (i)   mask, role: character played by actor.
  (ii) legal connotation: someone with title to property
  (iii) concrete individual: that which distinguishes me
        from another, that which makes me me.

The word person has a very different meaning for the twenty-first-century individual than it did within the arguments of the first five centuries. In the context of the early Councils, *person* does not mean psychological centre and cannot be interpreted in terms of the personality, ego, etc. One must avoid any later post-Freudian overtones: to say God *is* Three Persons is not to claim God *has* three personalities.

Very closely associated with *prosōpon* in Greek thought is the word *hypostasis* (Greek: plural: *hypostaseis*) which answers the question, 'Who is this particular person in all his/her individuality?' 'This is John and none other'; 'This is Mary and none other.' This word can be interpreted in two ways:

(i) 'that which underlies', substratum, 'metal underlying the gilt', content, 'stuff from which something is made' (i.e. inner being, inner content). On this reading, *hypostasis* means the substance of God, equivalent to *ousia* (the understanding of the Latin West: *hypo-stasis = sub-stantia* – God is one *hypostasis*).

(ii) 'that which gives support', buttress, prop, the thereness of something, concrete expression as opposed to theory, existence of something, this rather than that (Eastern understanding). On this reading, *hypostaseis* are understood as representing the *three* divine persons: that which distinguishes, but neither separates, nor divides the divine persons from each other.

In West *hypostasis* was generally translated as substance (Latin: *substantia*). Using this interpretation of the term the Western theologians became increasingly worried that the East was teaching a doctrine of three *hypostaseis* understood as three separate divine substances i.e. tritheism (a doctrine of three separate Gods). It was not until the later fourth century that the West realised that *hypostasis* had two meanings and that (ii) was the usual one. The part played by Athanasius and Hilary is important here, the former travelling West on a number of occasions, the latter travelling East.

The Aftermath of Chalcedon
The Council had produced a compromise statement acceptable to the West fitting comfortable with the language of Augustine:

> This is that ineffably accomplished sole taking up of man by God the Word, so that he might truly and properly be called at the same time the Son of God and the Son of man – Son of man on account of the man taken up, and the Son of God on account of the God only-begotten who took him up, so that a Trinity and not a Quaternity might be believed in.[9]

For the most part, this settlement survived the vicissitudes of western disagreement and remained acceptable to the major churches even after the turmoil of the Reformation.

---

9. Augustine, *The Predestination of the Saints*, in P. Schaff, *Saint Augustine: Anti-Pelagian Writings, The Nicene & Post-Nicene Fathers of the Christian Church*, First Series, T&T Clark, Edinburgh, 1997, p. 513.

The Creed of Chalcedon (451)

Following then the holy Fathers, we all with one voice teach
that it should be confessed
that the Lord is *one and the same Son* [against Nestorians]
the same perfect in Godhead, the same perfect in manhood,
the same truly God and truly man,
of *a rational soul* and a body [against Apollinarians]
homoousios with the Father as to his Godhead,
homoousios with us as to his manhood;
in all things like unto us, sin only excepted;
born of the Father before the ages as to his Godhead,
and the same, in the last days, for us and for our salvation,
[born] of *Mary the Virgin Theotokos* as to his manhood.

One and the same Christ, Son, Lord, Only-begotten,
made known in two natures,
without confusion, without change [against Monophysites],
without division, without separation [against Nestorians];
the difference of the two natures having been in no way
taken away by reason of the union,
but rather the properties of each being preserved
[against Monophysites],
and both concurring into *one prosōpon* and *one hypostasis*
not parted or divided into two *prosōpa* [against Nestorians]
but one and the same Son and Only-begotten,
the divine Logos, the Lord Jesus Christ [the main Alexandrian stress]
as the prophets taught from the beginning concerning him
and as Jesus Christ himself taught us,
and the creed of the Fathers handed down to us.

For the most part, this settlement survived the vicissitudes of western disagreement and remained acceptable to the major churches even after the turmoil of the Reformation.

In the East, the Council of Chalcedon left many uneasy. It was felt that its creed had sacrificed the position of Cyril and the Council of Ephesus and left the way open for a resurgence of Nestorianism. As with the period following all councils of the church, the next hundred years was a time of tension and confusion, party fighting against party. A second council of Constantinople (553) tried to steer the church into accepting a much more radical, and ultimately unacceptable, Alexandrian position. It was left to the third Council of Constantinople (680–1) to restore the balance, upholding the western insistence on the full humanity of the Lord Jesus Christ and establishing the unity of the divinity and humanity of Christ at the level of one common *hypostasis*, hence faith's acceptance of what is familiarly entitled the doctrine of the hypostatic union.

In Asia, with the remarkable rise of the Moslem caliphates in Syria, and later in Mesopotamia, the Eastern Empire was now facing destruction. The settlement achieved by Constantinople III was less successful and the fractures still remain in need of healing, a fact attested by the sensitivities surrounding rights of occupation to the church of the Holy Sepulchre in Jerusalem even today. Chalcedonian christology was accepted by the eastern imperial power, the Melkites (Hebrew/Syriac *melek*, the king's party), but large parts of the provinces broke away from this solidarity of faith, eventually coming together in two groups: the five oriental churches (Armenian, Coptic, Syrian [Jacobite], Ethiopian and Indian [Malankara]) tending towards monophysite in their allegiance; and the Assyrian church, spreading across the Lebanon, Syria, Iraq and Iran and preserving a tradition originating with the Nestorian party. Both churches flourished, the latter developing a missionary endeavour in southern India and through Persia into Turkestan and along the silk route into Northern China, where in Sianfu the seventh century Nestorian stone represents the most easterly monument of early Christianity. These flourishing churches suffered grievously with the rise of Islam and huge areas of the east were lost to Christianity.

As the unity of the ancient Roman Empire came to an end, divisions between the churches hardened around long-treasured formulae, in Latin, Greek, Syriac and Coptic and the rest. Communities were cut off from one another, increasingly divided by language and changing customs. The beliefs held by many groups were far closer to others than they often understood, but they drifted apart. It is only now that we can again seek to learn from one another's insights, and begin to break down the divisions in Christ's family as we struggle once again to profess with one voice our common belief in One Lord and One Church.

CHAPTER SIX

Protocols against Idolatry

Through Christ to the Father

The series of christological councils from the fourth to the seventh centuries, which I explored briefly in the preceding chapter, provided a framework for an approach to the mystery of the Word made flesh (Jn 1:14). They provided a true exposition of the texts of the New Testament but, at the same time, point to the saving acts of God in Jesus, not simply as something to be recalled from the past, but as a present reality in the lives of the Christian community. Matthew's gospel recalls a saying which expresses this perfectly: 'Where two or three are gathered in my name, I am there among them' (Mt 18:20). The doxology at the end of the Eucharistic Prayer, already present in the oldest known example of the Eucharistic Prayer, that of Hippolytus of Rome (early third century), also preserves a central doctrinal insight: 'Through him, with him, and in him, in the unity of the Holy Spirit, all glory and honour is yours Almighty Father, for ever and ever. Amen.' There is an inevitable ordering (*taxis*) in our relationship with God. Our worship and our activity is directed to God the Father, here and now, through the present reality and mediation of Jesus Christ, living, as we do, in the all-embracing mystery of the Holy Spirit. Although the historical Jesus is to be identified with the risen Christ, we are saved from anything which might resemble a cult of Jesus, because in Jesus we encounter the mystery of God in the reality of our lives. Jesus is not the focus of our worship, God is. Herbert McCabe can thus rightly claim:

> It would be to betray a tritheistic rather than a trinitarian view to imagine that the New Testament records the coming of the Son instead of the coming of the Father. In Jesus we have the visitation of Yahweh of which the prophets spoke. The word of God is the way in which the Father sees himself, his realisation of himself; the incarnation means that this divine self-realisation is

89

shared with us. We are able to enter into the language, and hence the life, of the Father.[1]

Language and God

At various times the classic christology of the Councils has been challenged as unhelpful offering merely various attempts to express the mystery of Christ in a collection of concepts which are out of date and incomprehensible to the modern world. This claim might be illustrated by the collection of essays edited some years ago by John Hick, *The Myth of God Incarnate*.[2] This volume offers a good example of an error which underlies many of our discussions concerning the mystery of the person of Christ. In treating the language of pre-existence, person, and nature as a now outdated mythology, the authors appear to be suggesting that such language is somehow descriptive, rather than normative.

The essays by Maurice Wiles outline the central theme of this book. The language of incarnation is simply a myth, something not literally true, but embodying a more profound interpretation about the meaning of life, of human suffering, sin, reconciliation, and human re-integration. Michael Goulder suggests that such mythical language belongs to a three-tier universe, heaven above, and hell below, with earth in the middle: in this context he describes incarnation, with remarkable crudity, 'a landing-take-off-and-landing myth'.[3] A new scientific understanding of the world makes nonsense, he suggests, of Christ's descent to earth and return to heaven. John Hick expressed his disappointment that the orthodox language of Nicaea and Chalcedon 'merely reiterated that Jesus was both God and man, but made no attempt to interpret the formula'. Such an idea without content 'remains a form of words without assignable meaning'.[4]

Language is more subtle than Hick allows. A form of words can point to something without necessarily offering a description of it. We can claim both appropriately and quite literally that 'God is good' without making any claims about what such an

---

1. Herbert McCabe, *Law, Love and Language*, Sheed and Ward, London, 1979, p. 126.
2. John Hick, *The Myth of God Incarnate*, SCM, London, 1977, p. 178.
3. Michael Goulder, 'The two Roots of the Christian Myth' in *The Myth of God Incarnate*, p. 80.
4. John Hick, 'Jesus and the World Religions' in *The Myth of God Incarnate*, p. 178.

expression might mean. Such a predicate, '... is good' is topic neutral, and can never be metaphorical because it has no primary significance as predicated of any subject term more literally than of any other.[5] This is saying something about the way words function, and not of what they apply to. In a similar way Hick argues that to claim 'the historical Jesus of Nazareth was also God is as devoid of meaning as to say that this circle drawn with a pencil on paper is also a square'.[6] The relationship between God and man is in a completely different category than that between circles and squares. Meanings can contrast with one another only within a common category: thus we can compare sheep with goats as different sorts of animals, circles with squares as different sorts of shapes.[7] God and human beings have nothing in common by which they can be compared. They do not occupy the same space, for God cannot be said to occupy any space:

5. Gilbert Ryle, 'Categories', in Antony Flew, ed., *Logic and Language*, Oxford University Press, Oxford, 1953, pp. 65–85.
6. John Hick, 'Jesus and the World Religions' in *The Myth of God Incarnate*, p. 178.
7. A delightful illustration of this is to be found in Edwin Abbott's *Flatland* (originally published by Seeley & Co, London, 1884, republished Penguin, Harmondsworth, 1998). This fable carefully depicts a two-dimensional world, 'flatland', in which true space is a plane, where the inhabitants can only see shapes in terms of lines, recognising the existence of angles, triangles, squares, polygons, and circles by hearing, by touch, or by inference. The flatland narrator dreams of 'lineland', a one-dimensional world in which space is merely length. The inhabitant of lineland cannot see anything apart from a point, detecting length only by sound, and voice is the essence of their being. Later the narrator dreams of pointland, a non-dimensional gulf. At one point in the story, our two-dimensional narrator encounters a three-dimensional sphere, something that can only be seen in his two-dimensional world as a straight line of varying length (the intersection of a sphere with a plane), but, by inference, recognised as a circle. In attempting to convince our flatlander of a three-dimensional universe, he struggles to explain by geometric and arithmetic progression the meaning of a cube. Eventually, after a number of different attempts to convince the flatlander of three-dimensional space, the sphere whisks him into three-dimensional space. To the horror of the sphere, our flatlander has the affrontery to dare to suggest the possibility of a land of four dimensions, which the former just cannot envisage, for he is as trapped in three-dimensional space as the linelander had been in one-dimensional space. Eventually, he tries to convince his fellow flatlanders of the possibility of a three-dimensional world, and is sentenced to perpetual imprisonment for his pains. This story, written some thirty years before Einstein's theory of General Relativity (1917), as well as Heisenberg and Schrödinger's work on quantum theory might give not only the physicist occasion to speculate on the possibility of other ways of conceiving reality, but also the theologian.

It follows that there is not, after all, the same contradiction in saying that Jesus is both man and God as there would be in saying that a circle is a square or that Jesus is both man and sheep. This does not mean that we actually *understand* what it means to say that Jesus is man and God; of course we do not clearly understand this any more than we clearly understand what it means to say God created the world ... The doctrine of the incarnation, like the doctrines of creation and redemption, is not conveying information, it is pointing to a mystery in Jesus.[8]

It is important to labour the point because if Hick and Wiles are correct, we can no longer talk in any way about the mystery of God.

One final example. In another essay, Frances Young makes the claim that atonement 'is a conviction that God has somehow dealt with evil ... yet, to say this kind of thing is to use poetic, anthropological or "mythological" language; it is not to present a theological conclusion based on logical argument.'[9] She can go on to say of the incarnation: 'To reduce *all of God* to a human incarnation is virtually inconceivable, a fact to which the Trinitarian language is the traditional response.'[10] It is hard to know what to make of this sort of language. Neither the first part of her claim, nor the second makes any sense. It is not only 'virtually inconceivable', it is nonsense to suggest that we can reduce *all of God* to a human incarnation; and, equally, that God can somehow be divided into parts. The traditional language of theology never sought to assert such an absurd claim. Similarly, salvation depends not on a subjective conviction that evil has been dealt with, but on the fact that as a result of salvation our relationship to God has been changed.

While not wishing to dismiss completely *The Myth of God Incarnate*, and accepting that it raises some interesting questions, my chief criticism lies in the fact that the essayists appear insensitive to the nuances of religious language, and totally misrepresent the language and terminology of the patristic period, which I have explored, all too briefly, in the last chapter. This is an error which is not uncommon today. It must be contested. The

---

8. Herbert McCabe, 'The Myth of God Incarnate', in *God Matters*, Mowbray, London & New York, 1987, p. 58.
9. Frances Young, 'A Cloud of Witnesses', in *The Myth of God Incarnate*, p. 35.
10. Ibid.

patristic writers were writers of great subtlety: they never took the language about God literally, but struggled hard to point to the fact of 'God in Christ reconciling the world to himself' (2 Cor 5:19) in words that marked out, rather than trespassed upon, the mystery.

Augustine and Aquinas on the Divine–Human Encounter in Christ
It is refreshing to turn from this group of writers to the letters of Augustine. Augustine's long letter to Volusianus, written in 412, for example, offers a reply to a discussion the latter relates in which he had been asked just 'how he whom the universe is supposed to be scarcely able to contain could be concealed within the small body of a crying infant?' Augustine replies that such questions are asked only by those 'who are incapable of conceiving anything but material substances'.[11] God was not so united with human nature that 'He either relinquished or lost the administration of the universe, or transferred to that body as a small and limited substance':

> God is not said to fill the world in the same way as water, air, and even light occupy space, so that with a greater or smaller part of himself he occupies a greater or smaller part of the world. He is able to be everywhere present in the entirety of his being: he cannot be confined in any place: He can come without leaving the place where he was: he can depart without forsaking the place to which he had come.[12]

Augustine goes on to establish the true humanity of Jesus which was assumed but not destroyed: 'the fact that he took rest in sleep, and was nourished by food, and experienced all the feelings of humanity ... became subject to the succession of the seasons, and the ordinary stages of the life of man. For his body which began to exist at a point of time, became developed with the lapse of time'.[13] In a passage echoing the one I have already quoted, Augustine talks of the union between the Word of God and Jesus:

---

11. Letter 137. 1. 2; 2, 4, in Philip Schaff, ed., *The Confessions and Letters of St. Augustine, The Nicene and Post-Nicene Fathers*, vol. 1. T&T Clark, Edinburgh, reprinted 1994. I am grateful to Professor Lewis Ayres for alerting me to this important letter (*The Tablet*, 20 February 2010, p. 28).
12. Ibid., 2.4.
13. Ibid., 2.4.

> Wherefore the Word of God, who is also the Son of God, co-eter-
> nal with the Father, the Power and the Wisdom of God, mightily
> pervading and harmoniously ordering all things, from the high-
> est limit of the intelligent to the lowest limit of material creation,
> revealed and concealed, nowhere confined, nowhere divided,
> nowhere distended, but without dimensions, everywhere pre-
> sent in His entirety, – this Word of God, I say, took to Himself, in
> a manner entirely different from that in which he is present to
> other creatures, the soul and body of a man, and made, by the
> union of Himself therewith, the one person Jesus Christ,
> Mediator between God and men, in his Deity equal with the
> Father, in His flesh, i.e. in His human nature, inferior to the
> Father, – unchangeably immortal in respect of the divine nature,
> in which He is equal with the Father, and yet changeable and
> mortal in respect of the infirmity which was His through partici-
> pation in our nature.[14]

This letter, written nearly seventy years before the Council of
Chalcedon, in its balanced rhetorical phrasing, and in its refusal
to attempt what cannot be said, sums up with austere elegance
the belief of the church. Thomas Aquinas, the great theologian
of the Middle Ages, allows us to tease out the implications of
this letter a little further.

Aquinas maps out the relationship between God and Christ
in three ways.[15] As in all other creatures, God relates to him as
Creator, upholding him in existence 'by essence, power and
presence' every moment of his life. Just as we belong to the particular world of the twenty-first century, Jesus belonged to first-
century Palestine with all its inevitable limitations. His knowledge and experience of God and the world was that of a Jewish
man of his time, just as ours is of our time.[16] God was also related
to Christ 'by sanctifying grace', a relationship which is granted
to all the saints. He has gifts of spiritual insight and is imbued

---

14. Ibid., 3.12.
15. Thomas Aquinas, *Summa Theologiae*, vol. 48, ed. R. J. Hennessey, Eyre &
    Spottiswoode, 1976, 3a, 2, 10, ad 2; for the next few paragraphs I follow John
    McDade's useful summary of Aquinas in 'Jesus in Recent Research', *The
    Month*, December 1998, pp. 495–505.
16. It is a central principle of interpretation for Thomas that *cognita sunt in
    cognoscente secundum modum cognoscentis* (*Summa Theologiae*, II–II, q. 1, a 2 'Things
    known are in the knower [known] according to the mode of the knower').

with the Spirit. This is an experience that can well be illustrated by looking at the lives of the saints. St Teresa of Avila, St John of the Cross, and in more recent times St Thérèse of Lisieux, and many others, testify to this. Thérèse Martin, for example, though brought up within the narrow confines of the harsh, yet senti-mental and unappealing piety of late nineteenth-century France, still marked as it was by the scars of Jansenism, was granted a profound insight into the mystery of God's love. Entering the Carmelite convent at fifteen and dying of the rav-ages of tuberculosis a mere nine years later she entered into the heart of that dark night of Godforsakenness and alienation which has shrouded the modern world, yet preserved a power-ful belief in God's mercy, making a self-offering to Merciful Love in 1895. Though only twenty-four when she died, and hav-ing made no formal study of theology, she was rightly pro-claimed a Doctor of the Church by John Paul II in 1997, a prophet for our own age.[17]

This Divine-human encounter is something experienced by human beings, contextualised as they are in a particular time and place. It can be none other for Jesus, though as one without sin, his human experience of the mystery of God must in-evitably be more intense than for those, called to holiness, but none the less with minds and wills darkened by sin. This is why the insistence of the last christological Councils remains so important and still stands as a clear guarantee that any under-standing of Christ which undermines his true humanity is ulti-mately a betrayal of what it means to be a Christian. The Council of Chalcedon (451) and the Third Council Constantinople (681) stood firm in asserting the church's belief in Christ's true and full humanity in the face of serious threats from both mono-physites (those who insisted that Christ had but one nature, that of the pre-existent Word of God) and later the monothelytes (those who insisted that Christ had but one will, that of the pre-existent Word of God). Robert Butterworth can argue that:

> Jesus, in a thoroughly human fashion, understood how he stood with God and with men [and that this] the source of the

---

17. There are many studies of St Thérèse: see, for example, Bernard Bro, *The Little Way*, DLT, London, 1997. For an excellent study of the Carmelite tradition see Noel O'Donoghue, *Adventures in Prayer*, Burns & Oates, London, 2008.

Christian revelation of God ... a new experience of God entered human history, an experience of God which indispensably involved the human as it first occurred to and found expression in the mind of Jesus. Believers in the God who thus revealed himself in Jesus and was experienced by Jesus in his own self-grasp would henceforth need to take steps both to preserve and promote that foundational revelation and experience. Among the steps taken was the gradual development of a christology that would keep Jesus central to the Christian faith and its characteristic experience of God.[18]

The normative nature of our encounter with the person of Jesus Christ
It is for this reason that an encounter with the person of Jesus, enshrined as it is in a living tradition of faith, remains normative for our experience of God in the world. The disciple of Christ is in the world as one who listens; as one who is prepared to learn. She listens to the still small voice of God in her heart and lived out in the experience of the tradition, but she also looks out to affirm the presence of the Spirit wherever the Spirit may be found. Indeed, the Spirit works through the church, but is not bound by the church: it blows where it will (Jn 3:8). We remember the great Reformation insistence of God's uncovenanted mercies. In a pluralist society it is, I believe, increasingly the task of the followers of Christ to stand out against anything that diminishes what it means to be human, and to affirm and support all those, who, in one way or another inspired by the Spirit, are working to promote the good of humanity. But we can go further than this: formed by the experience of Christ mediated by the tradition, we are in a position to discern and proclaim the Spirit of God working not only in other individuals, but other communities and faith traditions.[19]

It is only after having established Aquinas' first two ways of accounting for the relationship between God and Christ, that we can turn to his third way: the personal union between God's Word and Jesus of Nazareth. Apart from asserting this fact, it is

---

18. Robert Butterworth, 'Has Chalcedon a Future?', *The Month*, April 1977, p. 112–13.
19. See Gavin D'Costa, 'Christ, the Trinity and Religious Plurality' in Gavin D'Costa and Paul F. Knitter, *Christian Uniqueness Reconsidered: Myth of Pluralistic Theology of Religions* (Faith Meets Faith Series in Interreligious Dialogue), Orbis Books, New York, 1990, pp. 16–29. Augustine makes a similar point in his Letter 137, 3. 12 (*The Nicene and Post-Nicene Fathers*, First Series, vol. 1).

hard to say anything further. It might be useful at this point to summarise Robert Butterworth's brief sketch of what Chalcedon was about. This Council insisted on the church's belief that Christ is no less God than the Father is God, no less human than we ourselves are; it goes on to insist that Jesus does not simply mediate a revelation of God, but reveals God by being the person he is and this inexpressible but essential unity is asserted in the Chalcedonian formula no less than eight times.[20] Butterworth insists:

> The oneness is strictly not a problem but a mystery. The duality of natures does not constitute the mystery, but rather exposes the shape of the problem that the revealing oneness of Jesus presents to the human mind.[21]

It needs to be reaffirmed that Chalcedon is not conveying information about the mystery of God, but rather mapping out how we may delineate and mark out an appropriate way of talking about that mystery. The language of the christological Councils contributes the linguistic rules of engagement; what is being said is normative, not descriptive.

Reticence in our talk about God

The inability of humans to speak adequately of God is a theme which pervades the writings of St Thomas Aquinas. The highest knowledge of God that we can attain to in this life is the admission that we are caught up in a cloud of unknowing. This was the hard discovery made by the Hebrew people. The first commandment makes harsh demands:

> You are forbidden to make an image of him by which you might wield numinous power, you are forbidden to invoke his name in magical rites. You must deny the other gods and you must not treat Yahweh as a god, as a power you could use against your enemies or to help you succeed in life. Yahweh is not a god, there are no gods, they are all delusion and slavery. You are not to comprehend God within the conventions and symbols of your own time and place; you are to have no image of God because the only image of God is man.[22]

---

20. Robert Butterworth, art. cit., p. 116.
21. Robert Butterworth, art. cit., p. 117.
22. Herbert McCabe, *Law, Love and Language*, Sheed and Ward, London, 1979, p. 119.

We are left with nothing to say. It is the achievement of the greatest and most private of love poetry, as of the best theology, to hint at something more. Thomas knew only too well that we must go on using words for, as finite and contingent beings, words are all we have. As he remarks in his commentary on John's gospel:

> God's indwelling whether by grace or by glory cannot be known except by experiencing it; it cannot be explained in words.[23]

So what is the use of words in our discourse about God? In one sense we use words to shape for ourselves what Nicholas Lash has appropriately termed 'protocols against idolatry'.[24] It is a theme Lash takes up in a slightly different way in his reflection on the creed, *Believing Three Ways in One God*:

> We learn to use this word (God) well, not by attempting to gain some purchase on God's nature, but by learning to live, and think and work and suffer, within the pattern of Trinitarian relationships which the creed supplies.[25]

He goes on to explore this point further:

> ... suppose then ... we turn the tables round and entertain the possibility that growth in understanding of the unknown God is to a large extent a matter of learning to put more of ourselves into everything we are and do, thereby becoming a little more alive and thus participating somewhat better in God's creative work.[26]

There can be no simple answer to the question about God, offered as it were from the outside. This is perhaps why St Ignatius Loyola, who was so deeply caught up in the mystery of the Trinity, set such store by the examen of consciousness. We can only fashion our language of God from within a pattern of human experiencing which gives shape to the words we use. We must be in touch with this experiencing. People might claim a belief in the Trinitarian God, but the important issue remains how that claim is to be given flesh and blood in life's encounters.

---

23. Thomas Aquinas, *In Joann. 1, lect 15,* cited by T.C. O'Brien, Appendix 3, *Summa Theologiae,* vol. 7, Eyre & Spottiswoode, 1976, p. 262.
24. Nicholas Lash, *Easter in Ordinary,* SCM, 1988, p. 104.
25. Nicholas Lash, *Believing Three Ways in One God,* SCM, 1993, p. 33.
26. Nicholas Lash, *Believing Three Ways in One God,* SCM, 1993, p. 37.

Such a comment might seem merely an attempt to change the terms of the discussion: to talk not of God but of humanity. But I do not think that this is the case. We all too easily think of our talk of relating to God as a question of talking about two beings in relation. Relation might be a way of expressing our utter dependence on God but we cannot be said to relate to God in the normal sense of the term relating. God is the ground of our existing; God is that without which nothing can be. As Teilhard de Chardin has it, God is *le milieu divin*: the divine field, that which is both the gracious centre of our life and the graced environment in which that life is lived out. In lighter vein, we may recall the parable of the fish searching for the meaning of the ocean, unaware of the water as something which was all around it, constituting its very environment and enabling it to exist. Such a medium is not only the medium of our existing but also the only possible medium of our talking and reflecting on that existence. We are reminded of this in Rupert Brooke's 'Heaven', that wry and somewhat irreverent poem of 1913: the metaphysical musings of a fish, searching for 'a Purpose in Liquidity', sees its fishy heaven constituted by a 'wetter water, a slimier slime'. And so it must always be: we have only the resources of own world to provide the language of metaphysical reflection.

Affective knowledge
The richest manner of human knowing is affective and demands the engagement of the whole person: as such it is effective and creative. The classical doctrine of God, abstract though it might initially appear, is such a form of knowledge. It allows us to map out a path because its starting point lies in our own experience of relating to one another. God is closer to us than our very being. Although Thomas insists that words cannot be used in the same way of ourselves as of God, we can in some way, hesitant though it might be, go on using words. We are not lost for words but the words we use of God cease to be descriptive, they turn us back on ourselves and our own experiencing. The American theologian, David Burrell, remarks that:

> We cannot pretend to offer a description of a transcendent object without betraying its transcendence. But reflecting on the

rules of discourse brings to light certain contours of discourse itself. And those outlines can function in lieu of empirical knowledge to give us a way of characterising what we could not otherwise describe.[27]

The doctrine of God reminds us that one of the rubrics which govern our talk of God is the concept of simplicity. God is God's attributes. This means that when we use adjectives in our talk of God they behave rather differently than they do in ordinary discourse. God is good, but God is also goodness itself. God is loving, but God is also love itself. God is wise, but God is also wisdom itself. God is Trinity. The theology of the Western Church loses something of the dynamic of Orthodox thought at this point in stressing the logical priority of the unity of God over the trinity of Persons. For the East, God's being is understood as the mutual relating of three persons, expressed by way of a most felicitous pun as a divine dance, or *perichoresis*. God is both communion and ground of all communion.

In the early chapters of this book I have tried to set out the New Testament evidence establishing the mystery of the person of Christ. The community's understanding of Christ is rooted in what Jesus said and did during his earthly ministry, his subsequent death, and resurrection. As they came to terms with the significance of his person, their belief was further shaped by their prayer and worship, as they gathered together for the celebration of the Breaking of Bread seeking to make sense of their experience by an engagement with the Hebrew scriptures. They found God in Christ, because in him they experienced salvation. It is in this context that we can begin to appreciate the formation of the New Testament texts. The writings of the Fathers, and the decrees of the Councils, attempted to say no more than had been said before, but provided norms by which the biblical texts could be interpreted accurately, while remaining true to the lived experience of the tradition. They discovered that the life, death, and resurrection of Jesus Christ, as it is mediated in the life-giving experience of the Spirit which forms the Christian community, allows us entry into the life of God. In the final two chapters of this book I shall try to explore how this

---

27. David Burrell, *Aquinas, God and Action*, Routledge & Kegan Paul, 1979, p. 7.

experience of salvation was understood in the course of the history of the community's life, responding to different needs at different times. This can never be simply a personal and private experience. We go to God in the company of others, and in turn, as St Paul tells us, our encounter with God reconciling the world to himself makes us ambassadors (2 Cor 5:18–20). It is the Christian's task to confront evil and injustice in the world wherever it may be found, and at whatever cost.

CHAPTER SEVEN

God in Christ reconciling the World to himself

New Testament Images of Atonement

As I suggested at the end of Chapter Five, the word atonement, the at-one-ing of God and humanity, is one of the few technical terms that the English language has contributed to theology. Unlike the creedal statements about God and Christ, which we have already looked at, Christians have never limited themselves to one interpretation of what we might understand by a doctrine of salvation. The New Testament texts invoke all sorts of metaphors from daily experience to spell out how this might be experienced.

Illustrations are taken from human relationships: Christ reconciles human beings with God (Rom 5:10–11; 2 Cor 5:18–21; Eph 2:16); Christ's obedience had brought to an end humanity's disobedience (Jn 6:38; Phil 2:7–8). The everyday degradations of the slave market provide the metaphor of redemption: Christ's buying back men and women from their slavery to sin (1 Cor 6:20; Col 1:13–14). Christ is thus our ransom (Mk 1:45; 1 Pet 1:18). The work of the healer introduces us to the metaphor of salvation (*salus*: wholeness, health), well illustrated by the gospel miracles. Images of warfare bring in the idea of Christ's victory over the powers of evil and the devil (Rom 7:23–25; 1 Cor 15:54–57; Col 2:15). The law court contributes the powerful forensic language of justification, being declared righteous (Rom 2:13; Gal 3:11; Phil 3:9), which is central to the thought of Paul, and which played such an important role in Reformation thinking.[1] To these we must add a

---

1. Bultmann distinguishes between the forensic use of the word and its ethical use, commenting, 'when it denotes the condition for (or the essence of) salvation, *dikaiosyne* [righteousness] is a forensic term. It does not mean any quality at all, but a relationship. That is, *dikaiosyne* is not something a person has as his own; rather it is something he has in the verdict of the 'forum' (= law-court – the sense of 'forum' from which 'forensic' as here used is derived) to which he is accountable. He has it in the opinion adjudicated to him by another,' Rudolf Bultmann, *Theology of the New Testament*, vol. 1, SCM, London, 1971, pp. 271–2.

metaphor taken from religious experience: Christ is the sacrifice which restores the relationship between God and humanity (1 Cor 5:7–8; Eph 5:2; Heb 7:27; 13:10–13). This is the wealth of imagery caught up and even enriched in the vast collection of hymns meditating on the passion of Christ through the ages.

It is instructive to note that in all these images the initiative is always in God's hands. It is God's love for us that is re-creative and makes us whole. There is no sense in any of these images that somehow humans have to placate an angry God. One of the central themes in classical discussions of christology lies in the fact that it is not simply what Christ does, but *who he is* that matters for salvation. As Pope Leo the Great has it: Christ 'entered into a bargain of salvation, taking upon himself what was ours and granting what was his'.[2] Sadly, in the West particularly, the emphasis increasingly focused on a concern with what Christ did, interpreted not only in terms of his life, death and resurrection, but more narrowly in terms of his death on the cross as the primary 'work of salvation'. Overemphasis on the language of sacrifice, originally just one metaphor among many, has perhaps contributed to this narrowing of perspective.

The Classic or Dramatic Theory

The period that immediately followed the formation of the New Testament, however, kept alive the multiplicity of imagery found in these texts, and added others, often increasingly bizarre. The re-uniting of humanity with God was seen as a great drama, Christ doing battle with the powers of evil to win for men and women their original freedom of being at one with God. Humans need to be ransomed from the power of evil and it is Christ who provides the ransom (Mk 10:45). For the seventh century Maximus the Confessor, Christ offered his flesh as bait, poisonous to the insatiable dragon, but medicine for human nature.[3] Augustine could even play with the image of the cross as a mousetrap,[4] and Gregory of Nyssa talk of Christ's humanity as the bait concealing the hook and its barb.[5] Rather more

---

2. Leo, *Sermons*, 54.4.
3. Maximus the Confessor, *Five Centuries*, 1.8–13.
4. Augustine, *Sermons*, Migne, *Patrologia Graeca*, 38.1210.
5. Gregory of Nyssa, *Catechetical Addresses*, chapters 21–4, Migne, *Patrologia Graeca*, 45.57–65.

comprehensively other teachers pictured the cross as a raft to which men and women cling as they escape the world's universal shipwreck.

Although the depiction of Christ's atoning work as a warrior engaging in battle is more familiar in the words of writers of the East, it is also represented in an Anglo–Saxon poem in a late tenth-century manuscript preserved at Vercelli. Some verses of the poem are already to be found carved on the great eighth-century stone cross at Ruthwell in Dumfriesshire:

Then the young Warrior,	God the All-Wielder,
Put off his raiment,	steadfast and strong;
With lordly mood	in the sight of many
He mounted the cross	to redeem mankind.
When the Hero clasped me	I trembled in terror,
But I dared not bow me	nor bend to earth;
I must needs stand fast.	Upraised as the Rood
I held the High King,	the Lord of heaven.
I dared not bow![6]	

The Dream of the Rood, a poem of over 150 lines, powerfully depicts the reflections of the Cross itself as Christ mounts it in the manner of a young Anglo–Saxon warrior engaging in battle. A similar dramatic model of the atonement is depicted in C.S. Lewis' moving and popular children's fable, *The Lion, the Witch and the Wardrobe*[7] as Aslan invokes a deeper magic in submitting himself as a victim to the White Witch in substitution for the boy, Edmund, and in turning backwards the course of death.

The Juridical Theory

At the beginning of the second millennium, such play of imagery was increasingly to disturb theologians. On the one hand, the apparent use of trickery to lure the forces of evil to their destruction seemed unbecoming in a doctrine of God, but similarly such dramatic imagery invariably reduced mankind to the role of bystanders like the Pevensie children watching from a distance in Lewis' tale. As Charles Wesley was to remind his congregation in one of the great Eucharistic hymns, 'Would the

---

6. *The Dream of the Rood*, translated by Charles Kennedy, *An Anthology of Old English Poetry*, Oxford, 1965.
7. Geoffrey Bless, 1950.

Saviour of Mankind/Without his people die?/No, to Him we all are join'd/As more than Standers by' (no. 131). We are not mere bystanders, but are caught up in the mystery of Christ's sacrifice.

Anselm, the Benedictine Archbishop of Canterbury, was to put humanity in the centre of the picture in his account of the doctrine of atonement (*Why God became Man* [*Cur Deus Homo?*], 1098). In its original form Anselm's account is as dramatic as the earlier imagery. Invoking the feudal notion of honour, he argued that God could only respond logically to the human fall from grace in one of three ways: by forgiving the human family; by punishing humanity; or by accepting satisfaction. For Anselm, only the last two of these options, however, would preserve human dignity. Humanity itself was incapable of rendering satisfaction because Adam's sin, in dishonouring the infinite God, could only be restored by an infinite recompense. This infinite, honourable recompense was to be found in the obedience of the man Christ on the cross, God in Christ reconciling the world to himself (2 Cor 5:19) by restoring humanity's due of honour to God.

By the sixteenth century, this picture of atonement was interpreted very differently. For the Reformers, no longer was the focus on God's honour, but on human punishment. Now Anselm's picture was associated with the notion of penal substitution, something alien to Anselm's thought: in the crucifixion, Christ is seen to be standing in for humanity to avert God's wrath and to take upon himself the punishment deserved by sin. Perhaps the plagues which ravaged Europe in the fourteenth century, reducing Europe's population by between a third and two-thirds, as well as the developing sense of guilt and disillusion which followed from them played their part.

The Exemplarist Theory

What was needed was a reassertion of God's love. Some later theologians, and in particular the great medievalist, Hastings Rashdall in his *The Idea of Atonement in Christian Theology* (1919), argue that this was provided by Peter Abelard, the *enfant terrible* of the Paris schools. Although Abelard wrote no explicit work on atonement, Rashdall argued that his work offered a profound insight into God's passionate love for the individual sinner and reveals Christ's death on the cross as the supreme example of love, presenting a summons to men and women to respond to this act of love. In his commentary on Paul's letter to the Romans, Abelard comments: 'The purpose and cause of the incarnation was that he might illuminate the world by his wisdom and excite it to love of himself.'[8] C.F.D. Moule illustrates this with a passage from Helen Waddell's novel, *Peter Abelard*. Abelard and Thibault come across a little rabbit caught in a trap:

> It lay for a moment breathing quickly, then in some blind recognition of the kindness that had met it at the last, the small head thrust and nestled against his arm, and died ...
> 'Thibault,' [Abelard] said, do you think there is a God at all? Whatever has come to me, I earned it. But what did this one do?'
> Thibault nodded.
> 'I know,' he said. 'Only – I think God is in it too.'
> Abelard looked up sharply.
> 'In it? Do you think it makes him suffer, the way it does us?' ...
> 'Thibault, do you mean Calvary?'
> Thibault shook his head. 'That was only a piece of it – the piece that we saw – in time. Like that.' He pointed to a fallen tree beside them, sawn through the middle. 'That dark ring there, it goes up and down the whole length of the tree. But you only see it where it is cut across. That is what Christ's life was; the bit of God that we saw. And we think God is like that because Christ was like that, kind, and forgiving sins and healing people. We think that God is like that for ever, because it happened once, with Christ. But not the pain, not the agony at the last. We think that stopped ...'[9]

Here is a moving meditation on Pascal's enigmatic exclamation, 'Jesus will be in agony until the end of the world.'[10] Abelard and his followers do not appear to offer a mechanism by which we can show that it is God's act which brings about our restoration and healing. There is no room here for the

---

8. Cited in F.W. Dillistone, *The Christian Understanding of the Atonement*, SCM, London, 1968, p. 325.
9. C.F.D. Moule, 'The Sacrifice of Christ' in *Forgiveness and Reconciliation*, SPCK, London, 1998. The passage comes from Helen Waddell, *Peter Abelard*, 1933, pp. 288–91.
10. Pascal, *Pensées*, ed. Louis Lafuma, J. M. Dent, London, 1960, § 739.

costliness of grace. All they can offer is that we should imitate Christ's supreme act of love: as he loves us, so should we love one another. As Augustine found in his confrontation with Pelagius, imitation is too superficial a category to deal with the mysterious solidarities of grace. 'It is all of God' (2 Cor 5:18).

Sacrifice
This is something clearly expressed in interpreting atonement in terms of sacrifice, something I have already touched on in Chapter Two. Arguing simply from the facts surrounding Jesus' execution by the Roman administration, it would be very hard to identify his death as a sacrifice. Yet this is what Paul and the compilers of the gospels do. As we have seen, this theme is already present in the primitive creedal statement preserved in 1 Cor 15:3, which Paul seems to have inherited from Palestinian Christians and most probably from the Jerusalem church itself.[11] It finds its most complete development in the New Testament in the letter to the Hebrews.

Sacrifice is an extremely complex and multi-textured phenomenon. With little thought, we presume an understanding of the word and its use. We are familiar with the horrific rituals of human sacrifice to be found in Maya and Aztec culture. It is all too easy to interpret such rituals according to our own perspective; to read into them horrors we just do not know were there.

We do not know how the Aztec and Mayan peoples approached such events, nor even how the victims themselves viewed their approaching death. We are in worlds alien and strange, and we are repulsed by things other societies would understand differently. The actions and symbols being invoked are opaque, sometimes fashioned over a long period of time, and including many levels of meaning. No sacrifice can be interpreted rightly in isolation from its symbolic and social context. Problems of interpretation abound, as we attempt to tease out the meanings associated with the complex symbolism invoked in ritual.

The late-medieval emphasis on penal substitution and an inter-related focus on sacrificial immolation as destruction of

---

11. See Martin Hengel, *The Atonement*, SCM, London, 1981, pp. 37–9.

the offering seriously skews our understanding of Christ's sacrifice as well as of the Eucharist. Eugène Masure's point is telling:

> if immolation meant only putting to death, the sacrifice of the Cross would have been performed on Calvary by the executioners – which is repugnant ... The death of Christ on Calvary is a sacrifice not in so far as it is a judicial murder carried out by executioners ... but in so far as it is the self-immolation of God's Son.[12]

This is the doctrine that the Council of Trent sought to express, but the Council can only be interpreted within the limitations of the given historical circumstances of Reformation debate. This results in effectively reducing interpretation of the meaning of the death of Christ to the confines of the language of sacrifice, whereas this is only one of many constellations of metaphors invoked by the scriptures to interpret this saving and life-giving death. Such a limitation is inappropriate, as any study of the atonement abundantly makes clear. Having acknowledged this, however, it is important to accept the fact that the Tridentine 'rhetoric of propitiatory sacrifice'[13] is remarkably non-prescriptive. Neither sacrifice itself, nor the meaning of propitiation is defined: the Council Fathers remained cautious in their refusal to endorse the teaching of any one school of thought, its words remaining open to the widest of interpretations.

Linked with images of penal substitution, the idea of sacrifice can lead us to very dangerous ground indeed. Calvin's taking up of Hebrews 9:22 ('without the shedding of blood there is no forgiveness of sins') as an interpretative rubric for his discussion of sacrifice illustrates this:

> God's righteous curse bars our access to him, and God in his capacity as judge is angry towards us. Hence an expiation must intervene in order that Christ as priest may obtain God's favour for us and appease his wrath. Thus Christ to perform this office had to come forward with a sacrifice. For, under the law, also, a priest was forbidden to enter the sanctuary without blood, that believers might know, even though the priest as their advocate,

---

12. Eugène Masure, *The Christian Sacrifice*, Burns, Oates & Washbourne, London, 1944, pp. 262–3.
13. David N. Power, *The Sacrifice We Offer*, T&T Clark, Edinburgh, 1987, p. 187; for a discussion of this phrase see pp. 146–50.

stood between them and God, that they could not propitiate God unless their sins were expiated.[14]

We can begin blasphemously to misinterpret the mystery of God as a god who punishes, a god who demands a victim. C.F.D. Moule, while taking the devastations of sin with absolute seriousness, makes clear, in a carefully argued essay, how the notions of quantitative justice and punishment play little part in the New Testament gospel of grace. In the realm of sin we remain in a world of rewards and punishments, but in God we find ourselves in a totally different realm: 'For sin pays a wage, and the wage is death, but God gives freely, and his gift is eternal life' (Rom 6:23 [New English Bible version]).[15] God is a God of love; true God can be no other. It is the forgiven sinner who changes, not God. As sinners, it is all too easy for us to misinterpret 'the wrath of God' (Rom 4:18). The phenomenon of the Doppler effect can provide a useful analogy: just as the light from a star moving away from an observer has a longer wavelength (redshift) than a star moving towards an observer (blueshift) so do the hues of God's passionate love take on a different tone depending on whether the sinner is fleeing from, or running into God's healing embrace, a theme brought out powerfully in Francis Thompson's *Hound of Heaven*:

> Is my gloom, after all,
> Shade of his hand, outstretched caressingly?
> 'Ah, fondest, blindest, weakest,
> I am he whom thou seekest!
> Thou dravest love from thee, who dravest me.'

E.E. Evans-Pritchard's classic work on deciphering the rituals of the Nilotic communities of the Nuer, or Victor Turner's studies on Ndembu ritual, reveal some of the complexities of trying to understand what is going on in ritual. An observer does not always see what a participant sees, nor does she interpret what she sees in the same way. How would we decipher a fragment of the film of major heart surgery if we knew nothing of the context? We could hardly guess that at least temporarily removing

---

14. John Calvin, *Institutio*, 2.15.6, cited F.W. Dillistone, p. 199.
15. C.F.D. Moule, *Essays in New Testament Interpretation*, Cambridge University Press, 1982, pp. 235–49; see especially p. 240.

a heart was something going on for the person's better health. Even in the accounts provided by the Hebrew scriptures, for which we have more information, interpretation remains far from easy. In the Passover and Covenant rituals, for example, the blood of the victim is not offered to God but is used as a sign of God's deliverance and liberation of his people. At times we have to admit, as Douglas Davies reminds us, that 'there can be no final answer to some of these questions involving blood, since powerful symbols of this kind often operate on several levels of meaning some of which may no longer be available to us ...'[16]

Evans-Pritchard seems very hesitant to allow talk of *vicarious* substitution: Occasionally in a thunderstorm a Nuer might throw away a bead, or wad of tobacco, with the intention that it might stand in as a substitute for themselves.[17] In the more formal sacrifice this does not seem to be the case. The gesture of laying a hand on the sacrificial cow highlights the identity be-tween the sacrifice and the sacrificer[18] – it is a matter of 'this is me', not 'this is instead of me'. After all God does not benefit from sacrifice: God owns all the cattle anyway and 'needs noth-ing and does not ask for anything'.[19] God merely receives the life, the Nuer retain the meat. Nuer rarely kill wild animals and sacrifice is generally the only time that meat is eaten, yet the feasting following a sacrifice, celebratory though it might be, and possessing considerable social significance, cannot be thought of as a communion meal integral to the sacrifice.[20] It is not unknown for a Nuer tribesman to criticise his fellow for sacrificing too often merely for the chance to eat meat.[21]

Evans-Pritchard sees the key to this in the notion of abneg-ation. Humans deprive themselves of something, but such is the identification between the sacrificer and sacrificial victim that the sacrifice becomes a drama playing out the inner life and in-tentions of the one who sacrifices. The act of sacrifice recon-ceives our way of dwelling in the world. Gifts are symbols of

16. Douglas Davies, 'An Interpretation of Sacrifice in Leviticus', *Zeitschrift für die Alttestametliche Wissenschaft*, 89, 3 (1977), pp. 395.
17. E.E. Evans-Pritchard, *Nuer Religion*, Oxford, 1977, p. 281.
18. Ibid., pp. 261–2.
19. Ibid., p. 283.
20. Ibid., p. 215.
21. Ibid., p. 263.

inner states and in this sense one can only give oneself. Yet the act of sacrifice allows a complex play of the symbolism of identification worked out in a set of ideas focused by representative, rather than vicarious, substitution. In sacrifice some part of the sacrificer dies with the victim (cow or cucumber): we part with a state of sinfulness, with an old state of existence. What occurs can be regarded as an absolution, re-birth to new life, or self-immolation.

When the disciples of Christ acknowledge his sacrifice in coming together to celebrate Eucharist they recognise 'a divine summons to unite [themselves], by prayerful participation and especially by Holy Communion, with the total self-dedication of Jesus Christ the Redeemer in his obedience unto death, even death on a cross'.[22] The sacrifice of the Head is also that of the Body: in the Eucharist, Christ's sacrifice is the church's sacrifice. John Calvin, following Augustine, expresses this most clearly:

> Christ is our mediator through whom we offer ourselves and all that we have to the Father … He is our altar, upon which we place our oblations, that whatever we venture, we venture in him. In a word, it is he that 'hath made us kings and priests unto God'.[23]

This has implications both at a personal and corporate level. The Eucharist is not to be regarded as a 'commodity' but as the performance of a grace-filled, transforming action. As those who have received the Eucharist, we are to be a eucharistic people: we are to live out Christ's sacrifice in the pattern of our lives. The Eucharist is incomplete and is a mandate to Christians to share his sufferings and, as Paul dares to claim, to make up in our own bodies what was lacking in his afflictions (Col 1:24). The rather bland dismissal, 'Go in the Peace of Christ', suggesting closure, at our modern eucharistic celebration curiously fails to catch the import of the medieval *Ite, Missa est*: that open-ended sending out of his people to disturb and challenge the world as models of Christ's redeeming presence. This is a presence which cannot be lived without cost; we are to take up our own cross in lives of sacrificial service.

---

22. John McHugh, 'The Sacrifice of the Mass at the Council of Trent', in S. W. Sykes, ed., *Sacrifice and Redemption, Durham Essays in Theology*, SPCK, London, 1991, pp. 157–81; passage cited p. 180.
23. John Calvin, *Institutio*, 4.18.17. Refer to Augustine, *City of God*, bk 10, Chapter Six.

Christ's sacrifice tells us in words that should be spoken only hesitatingly that love is a costly business, and that God is prepared to bear the cost. I have dwelt in rather more detail on the image of sacrifice for its misinterpretation still dangerously, and often unconsciously, works to undermine our understanding of a loving God. The interpretation of sacrifice which I have offered also differs from the earlier models of atonement, especially when linked to the ritual of the Eucharist, invites us to contribute our own engraced involvement and witness to Christ's redeeming work.

Restorative Justice

My final image for atonement allows a similar human involvement. Traditionally, the figure of justice is depicted as blind, weighing the evidence in her scales; fair, because abstract and utterly impersonal. This is one of the underlying principles of our criminal system. The punishment fits the crime and society demands that the criminal should make retribution, paying his just deserts. It is an image that, like it or not, often colours our projection of God's justice. In recent years many communities have explored a different model of justice, both personal and far from being abstract, now known as restorative justice. It has proved highly creative in many conflict situations and programmes based on this process have been invoked in schools, local communities and even in criminal justice to great success. We are familiar to it in the remarkable healing brought about by the Truth and Reconciliation Commission in South Africa.

In the traditional scheme of things, justice is about punishing offenders for committing an offence against the state; restorative justice brings victims and offenders face to face in order to find positive solutions to crime by a process of encouraging offenders to face up to their actions, and make some sort of amends by restoring what was damaged. More significantly, the process demands that an offender should personally acknowledge the seriousness of what he or she has done and accept responsibility for their actions. By talking through the experience the victim can make the offender realise just how the offence has affected them, and is in a position to offer forgiveness. Far from being a soft option, as conversations with those in prison reveal, restorative justice is hard and very demanding: many offenders find it extremely difficult to face up to the impact of their crime. The easy option is to see a crime as impersonal, something abstract, an offence against the system, and, though I am falling into caricature, when caught it is often accepted as a fair cop, part of the game.

In the context of the traditional model of justice, the sheer gratuitousness of forgiveness can, in some minds, appear to trivialise the horror of sin. It is something our own generation particularly does not always take seriously enough. God takes on the cost of forgiveness and we appear to get off scot-free. But this is not true: 'Whereas the suffering involved in a reconciliation is almost infinitely intensified, it is never, when we stand inside the gospel, *retributive* suffering.'[24] As C.F.D. Moule comments in another place:

> The predicament of man cannot be met by a mere cease fire, or by a mere decision, like a 'royal pardon', to ignore the wrong. Sin has got to be taken account of ... Quantitative metaphors are recognized by the New Testament. And the good news is that the slack is taken up (so to speak) by God himself, in Jesus Christ; or, if I may again resort to that physiological metaphor, the lesion of the body's tissue can be healed only by the output of creative energy. It is a sovereign act of the Creator.[25]

This is surely the point. Restorative justice adds the missing dimension: the costliness of truly accepting the reality of forgiveness:

> On both sides, the sheer pain, emotional and psychological, is likely to be acute. The process is emphatically 'penal' in a literal sense. Forgiving is costly, and so is repenting.[26]

H.R. Macintosh seeks to spell this out in the context of the Christian life:

> He (the Christian) may well be obliged to face the shattering discovery that all his moral efforts are vain and that, in the light cast by God, he now appears even to himself as one who,

---

24. C.F.D. Moule, *Essays in New Testament Interpretation*, p. 248.
25. Ibid., p. 258.
26. C.F.D. Moule, 'Retribution or Restoration?' in *Forgiveness and Reconciliation*, SPCK, London, 1998, pp. 41–7; passage cited p. 43.

guiltily and unconditionally, has failed. In Christ's presence he learns, gradually or suddenly, the final truth about himself; and the revelation breaks him ... Nor will any message of reconciliation suffice which does not contain a relief for this, our profoundest and sorest need.[27]

Forgiveness cannot be earned. It can only be given freely. This is what is so devastating about it. For all its pain, however, for the one forgiven the moment can be creative, offering, enfolded as it is in grace, a new healing, but a healing not without its own cost. This is the realisation discovered by the Soul in Newman's *Dream of Gerontius*. The Angel of the Agony sings:

> O happy suffering soul! For it is safe,
> Consumed, yet quickened, by the glance of God.

And as the Soul in silence encounters the mystery of God's presence, it is the Soul himself who turns away, and pleads for purgation:

> Take me away, and in the lowest deep
>   There let me be,
> And there in hope the lone night-watches keep,
>   Told out for me.

Restoration in the Eastern Tradition

That Christ restores us to our full human stature as human beings called to live out our lives in the freedom of God's love is a theme rather more to the fore in the theology of the Eastern church. The Eastern church has a rather different approach to sin and the atonement than that found in the unfolding experience of the West, moulded as it has been by Saint Augustine's powerful reflections on the Fall. Augustine dramatically plays up the significance and responsibility of Adam, a perfect human being in a perfect world. Adam's disobedience is understood as an almost Sartre-like act of freedom and choice, free from any limitation or extenuating circumstances.[28] The Fall fractures human nature and relationships and sends shock

---

27. H.R. Mackintosh, *The Christian Experience of Forgiveness*, James Nisbet, London, 1927, p. 228; cited Dillistone, p. 300.
28. I am thinking of Mattieu's position at the end of the third volume of *Les Chemins de la liberté*.

waves throughout creation. Irenaeus represents a very different view. The key here is growth and maturation: just as in nature things begin as seedlings only attaining their perfect form at the end, so it is with human beings. Adam, at the beginning, is still at the stage of childhood, a weak and puny being, and sins as a result of this weakness and vulnerability, Satan bearing the greater responsibility. The emphasis changes. A preoccupation with Christ's reconciling death is replaced by the understanding that as Christ shared our flesh so that flesh becomes the flesh of divinity. Irenaeus could claim: 'For it was for this end that the Word of God was made man, and he who was the Son of God became Son of Man, that man, having been taken into the Word, and receiving adoption, might become the Son of God.'[29] Athanasius followed the same line, though he is rather more succinct in his daring remark: 'He, indeed, assumed humanity that we might become God.'[30] By sharing our lot, Christ is the healer who makes us whole. We were created in the image of God, an image lost by sin, but restored in Christ.

This powerful vision of human growth is delightfully and movingly explored in Margery Williams' little story, *The Velveteen Rabbit*.[31] It is a tale of a child's stuffed rabbit becoming so special to the child that, having been knocked about, lost in the garden, and having something of the stuffing knocked out of it, becomes 'real' to that child. The story makes the point that becoming real is a result of being loved into life. It is sometimes a long and painful process 'not for people who break easily, or have sharp edges, or who have to be carefully kept'.[32] This is God's dealing with us: we, too, are loved into life, and the brokenness of sin and its painful healing is part of this process.

This discussion of atonement has perhaps been rather different from the preceding chapters of the book in so far as it has been much more impressionistic, offering various images from biblical times up to the present day. One of the strengths of this approach to the doctrine has been that the community of the

---

29. St Irenaeus, *Against Heresies*, bk 3, 19.1 in *The Anti-Nicene Fathers*, vol. 1, eds Alexander Roberts and James Donaldson, T&T Clark, Edinburgh, 1996.
30. St Athanasius, *On the Incarnation*, Mowbray, London, 1953, § 54.
31. Margery Williams, *The Velveteen Rabbit*, Carousel Books, London, 1982.
32. Ibid., p. 9.

church never opted for one interpretation to the exclusion of others. It is clear that our response to God's saving love has been re-fashioned according to the needs of different societies. We can compare the various metaphors invoked in the doctrine and learn both from their strengths and limitations while at the same time responding to God's unique call to each of us, enfolded as we are in grace, to be drawn away from the confines of sin and fulfil his call. In Christ we become the people we were created to be.

CHAPTER EIGHT

Called to Communion in God

Putting on Christ

The lives of the men and women who first encountered Jesus were turned upside down by their experience. In him they found a new understanding of what it meant to be loved by God. They discovered an intimacy in the prayer of Jesus through which they could learn to experience God as Abba, Father: they felt God's nurturing and motherly care for men and women who felt themselves to be outcasts. In such experiences they could see the world anew. Not that they were suddenly offered an easy answer to everything. Life was still tough and brutal. The lives of many of the first generation of Jesus' companions were to end in torture and violent death. Yet somehow they were enabled to reconfigure their priorities. Their understanding of themselves, their view of the world, was called into question and challenged (what the gospels call *metanoia* [Greek: change of mind, about turn] Mt 4:17). In their relationship with Jesus these men and women had discovered what it meant to be made the recipients of love, forgiveness and compassion, and they longed to share this experience of God's healing with others.

As we attempt to answer Jesus' question to his disciples: 'Who do you say that I am?', Jesus turns the tables on us, and we find ourselves wrestling with the question, 'Who does Jesus say that I am?' Jesus challenges us to discover our full stature as human beings. The freedom with which he addressed women in the gospels, for example, his prioritising of the marginalised and those who were in any way oppressed, his call to sinners, all these reveal his determination to stand firmly against anything which diminished what it is to be fully human. Jesus was not afraid to transgress constraints imposed by contemporary social expectations in order to allow people to discover a richer way of celebrating their humanity.

Jesus' approach to his contemporaries has borne great fruit in recent years allowing women and men first to identify, and then to begin, the long process of challenging unjust structures in society, politics, and human relationships. Christians believe that a lived out christology offers the way to human freedom, allowing us to dream dreams, and to give flesh and blood to human aspirations. So very often, however, even the community of Christians has colluded with society and has allowed itself to be used 'to keep people in their place'. The infamous verse in Mrs Alexander's hymn 'All things bright and beautiful' might well have been excised from our hymnbooks,[1] but it is harder to heal the hurts and damage such unchristian values have done to society. New movements in Christian thought have begun the task. In an attempt to interpret the message of Vatican II (1962–5) within the poverty-stricken and oppressed communities of Latin America, liberation theology emerged to give a powerful voice to the voiceless. It has borne fruit in other countries, too. Movements in feminist theology have empowered women to rediscover their giftedness as the first witnesses of the resurrection in a church community diminished by male domination. Such theologies return human experience to a central location for the working out of christology.

Right believing and right living
The Western church has been challenged by the churches of the developing world to test its orthodoxy (Greek: *orthos* [upright, correct]; *dokeō* [to think, believe,]) its right believing, by right living or orthopraxis (Greek: *orthos* [upright, correct]; *praxis* [activity]), meaning right action. One cannot have the one without the other. Indeed actions come first: 'It is not those who cry out "Lord, Lord" who will be saved, but those who do the will of my Father' (Mt 7:21). Our pattern of life must show what it means to believe; we cannot just talk about belief.

Theologians in South America, Asia and Africa wishing to proclaim the meaning of Jesus in words which speak both to –

---

1. The rich man in his castle,
   The poor man at his gate,
   God made them high or lowly,
   And order'd their estate.

and from – the heart of the lives of the poverty-stricken communities which they serve, rightly insist that christology fails in its task if it finds expression merely as a form of words. Christology cannot remain untouched by the complex political and economic issues which oppress both individuals and communities. Our faith must be lived out in a pattern of authentic living, starting from the situation in which people actually live out their lives.[2] As Newman was to point out so vividly, with a near existentialist passion, doctrine does not unfold logically and neatly like a set of propositions or geometric equations. It follows from this that 'Many a man will live and die upon a dogma: no man will be a martyr for a conclusion.'[3] Doctrine is a principle of action and demands passionate engagement. It is a feature of the life of the church, a response to love: the human being 'is *not* a reasoning animal, he is a seeing, feeling, contemplating and acting animal'.[4]

The pattern of our lives must show something of our attempts to make sense of this thing we call living and to support and affirm others in their strivings to make sense. As the first letter of Peter tells us, it is a matter of giving 'an account of the hope that is within us'.[5] This is spelt out in words revealed by the way we live shaped, in turn, by the faith we express in our prayers and doctrine. Our primary task is not to offer answers, but rather to accompany others in their joys and sorrows, their doubts and fears; it is to be with others in risking our own precarious certainties. We bear witness. This journeying is often a journeying without words; assurance is found in a touch, a glance, too deep for utterance. This is expressed in a whole range of interrelated experiences: relationships, thoughts, yearnings, regrets, actions, mistakes, joys, fears, doubts, are bound together in a pattern which forms a rich, complex, and ever-renewed kaleidoscope of fragments.

---

2. See, for example, Jon Sobrino, *Christology at the Crossroads*, SCM, London, 1978; Gustavo Gutierrez, *A Theology of Liberation*, SCM, London, 1974; Juan Luis Segundo, *The Liberation of Theology*, Gill & Macmillan, Dublin, 1977.

3. John Henry Newman, *Grammar of Assent*, Longmans, Green & Co., London, 1924, p. 93.

4. Ibid., p. 94.

5. 1 Peter 3:15.

A Pattern of Existence

There can be no ready-made answer 'from outside'. A genuine answer must be shaped and tested by a lifetime of experience. When we recite the Creed we are proclaiming our belief in a new way of being human which we intend to express in a new way of living. A Christian's concern for matters of poverty, for community issues, for local justice, is not an added extra but a central expression of what it means not only to follow Christ, but also to the way in which we give shape to belief in Christ. Our belief in Christ is spelt out in our involvement with agencies such as the Catholic Fund for Overseas Development (CAFOD), or Progessio, and the like.

It is not inappropriate to understand this as a threefold, Trinitarian, pattern of existence, lived out in a constantly shifting pattern. This is particularly the case in giving flesh and blood to our understanding of Christ. We see, judge and act concerning relationships and events in the world around us. True seeing leads us to be more attentive to the needs of our brothers and sisters and of our environment and so to reflect. This leads in turn to decisions about what we should do, which demand inevitably that we act and which again brings us to reflect. All these are working for the kingdom to shape our present world according to the threefold pattern of the Trinity.

A real and lived-out relationship with God, the ground of our being, allows us to be more attuned and attentive to the needs of those around us. The discipline demanded of a disciple is not a living out of our lives according to a set of carefully honed rules, but offers the freedom of travelling light. Thomas Merton's comments about monastic discipline refer equally to the life of all disciples. There comes a point in all our lives when we have to accept the scary maturity involved in:

> the loneliness and disorientation of one who has to recognise that the old signposts don't show him his way, and that in fact he has to find his way by himself without a map. True, the monastic [or Christian] life provides other signposts and other maps: but the trouble is that too often the signposts point merely to a dead end and the maps are like those curious constructions of fourteenth-century cartographers which inform us that 'here be many dragons'. The real function of discipline is not to

provide us with maps, but to sharpen our sense of direction so
that when we really get going we can travel without maps.[6]

Prayer, says the Irish theologian, Enda McDonagh, 'is the
way we let God loose in the World';[7] it offers that disturbing call
to a way of life which offers an 'invitation to be vulnerable for
others'.[8] We are led to a deepening of understanding by a growing sensitivity which allows us to engage with how others see
things whether they be our own contemporaries or those who
have struggled to model Christ in different times and places.
Having reflected on the situation around us we are called to act.
We need to discern what actions constitute believing in Christ in
this world of ours. What activities allow us to bring healing and
consolation? What takes us out of the rut of our narrow
complacency and challenges us to ever-widening horizons as
men and women struggle for liberation in its most profound
sense? What actions are, for us and our fellows, foretastes and
sacraments of the reign of God? God did not reveal God's self
simply as an intellectual exercise, but in order to save us by
helping us to transform our lives in and through his love.

Being in Christ

The debates that so stirred the early church might seem, at first
sight, much less relevant today, their language dry and unnec-
essarily technical. I have attempted to show in Chapter Six
how such discussion remains important. The discussions of the
past, and especially the great debate about the person of Christ
which dominated the first seven centuries of the Christian era,
dramatise the questions that Christians must face today as they
struggle to make sense of their own lives and relationships.

As St Paul proclaims it, our life is to be 'in Christ' (e.g. Rom
8:1). We are called not only to a proclamation of the kingdom
but in Christ, we are invited to share the life of the Trinity. God
is closer to us than our very selves. St Thomas explores this
indwelling of all creatures in their gracious and divine ground

---

6. Thomas Merton, *Contemplation on a World of Action*, Image Books, New York,
   1973, pp. 126–7.
7. See, Enda McDonagh, *Doing the Truth*, pp. 40–57.
8. Edward Schillebeeckx, *Christ, The Christian Experience in the Modern World*,
   SCM, London, 1980, p. 229.

in what must be regarded as one of the high points of the *Summa Theologiae*: question 43. Thomas argues that 'God is in everything by his essence, power and presence.'[9] When discussing intelligent being, however, he suggests that we must point to an additional appropriation of presence 'in whom God is said to be present as the known in the knower and the loved in the lover … and by these acts of knowing and loving the intelligent being touches God himself'. In commenting on this theme, T.C. O'Brien, the editor of this volume in the Eyre & Spottiswoode edition of the *Summa Theologiae*, refers the reader to Thomas's commentary on Paul's second letter to the Corinthians in which Thomas argues that God is present in all things by God's own act in so far as he creates and sustains all things but that he is in the sanctified by *their* own acts in so far as they are able to know God and love God.[10] Thomas, echoing Augustine, dares to adopt the language of the lover, in a way quite as startling as that found in the later poems of John of the Cross. Thomas claims that we 'possess' God: God 'is at our disposal to use or enjoy as we wish'.[11] Dwelling in grace, we 'possess the power to rest joyfully in a divine person'. There is an 'enlightening of the mind', 'a kindling of the affections'.

It is important to remind ourselves that this breathtaking vision is played out in the pattern of the most ordinary experiences of our daily living. Without this divine ground we could not experience human love. We could not wonder at a great piece of music, or artistic creation. We would not be hurt by the fracturing of human relationships. At the same time, it is in reflecting on these human experiences that we are led to encounter God. Thomas, however, demands that we discriminate. We are called to embark on a process of discernment. The Son's presence to the mind is thus not reflected in the amassing of knowledge, an increase of facts, but in a deepening of insight, a quickening of the attention to the people and world that is taking shape around us.

---

9. Thomas Aquinas, *Summa Theologiae*, Eyre & Spottiswoode, vol. 7, 1976, ed. T.C. O'Brien, Ia 43, 3.
10. In 2 Cor 6, lect. 3, cited *Summa Theologiae*, vol. 7, 1976, ed. T.C. O'Brien, Eyre & Spottiswoode, London 1976, Appendix 3, p. 260.
11. *Summa Theologiae*, Ia 43, 3.

Thomas alerts us to the fact that in talking of such an immediate encounter we are best served by that range of metaphors associated with taste. Sight is too dispassionate a category to do justice to the demanding and enfolding delicacy of such an engagement. In a remarkable passage St Thomas Aquinas affirms:

> That a divine person be sent to someone through grace, therefore, requires a likening to the person sent through some particular gift of grace ... The Son is the Word; not, however, just any word, but the Word breathing Love ... Consequently not just any enhancing of the mind indicates the Son's being sent, but only that sort of enlightening that bursts forth into love ... So St Augustine says pointedly *the Son is being sent whenever someone has knowledge or perception of him,* for perception is a kind of experiential awareness and this is precisely what wisdom is, a knowing that, as it were, is tasted.[12]

Thomas insists that we truly become like the Son as we grow in wisdom; as we grow in sensitivity to one another; as we persevere in prayer; as we share with our sisters and brothers in the sacramental life of the church; as we struggle to discern the demands of the moral life. It is something that is worked out in the most ordinary experiences and encounters of daily living.

We are called to find God not merely by celebrating God's wonderful works revealed in scripture and in the pattern of creation, but in the heart of that unique mystery that makes us the people we are, and in those relationships which shape our lives. Good actions give us a knowledge of God. We savour the Word as we discover the delights of wisdom, just as when we alight on the mysteries of love we taste of the presence of the Spirit. For the classical doctrine of God there are two processions in the Trinity but underlying these two processions we are led to the elusive depths of a God who remains always unoriginate origin. We are led back to joy. Joy always comes to us from the outside, so to speak. It puts us in touch with the mystery of creativity. It is something which we experience in responding: that capacity to see the world as gift, gloriously and gratuitously unpredictable. This is that 'deep power of joy' through which 'we see into the life of things',[13] which we encounter in the

---

12. *Summa Theologiae,* 1a, 43, 5.
13. William Wordsworth, 'Lines composed a few miles above Tintern Abbey'.

poetry of Wordsworth as well as in the sermons and diaries of John Wesley. Here lies the discovery that our world can be experienced only as something given and that God can ultimately only be found in the mystery of gift, a gift received, a gift shared.

Seeing Lovingly

It is perhaps appropriate to explore this theme by turning briefly to the work of the novelist for the novelist contributes towards that deepening of insight which facilitates our spiritual journey. The work of Iris Murdoch, in particular, demands that we concern ourselves with the sheer intractability and elusiveness of the ordinary business of living. Iris Murdoch invokes the work of Simone Weil to explore that refocusing of the attention which is central to the experience we call prayer. We must learn to surrender our will, our desire to impose our own pattern and interpretation, and to allow ourselves to be called back from fantasy to confront the way things actually are in the world:

> It is in the capacity to love, that is to *see*, that the liberation of the soul from fantasy consists. The freedom which is a proper human goal is the freedom from fantasy, that is the realism of compassion.[14]

Iris Murdoch would argue that this seeing lovingly is a secular experience. Perhaps it is particularly important in the late twentieth century to explore this notion in a way that does not rely on the more traditional religious discourse. We have been arguing throughout this discussion that to believe in the Trinity is not a thing that Christians do merely in so far as they are Christians but in so far as they are humans wrestling with what it means to make sense of the world around them. For the Christian, it is precisely in the ordinariness and intractability of our human experience that we sense a capacity for loving fellowship which finds its response in the language of the Trinity. This is how we experience the nature of reality.

In so many of her novels Iris Murdoch provides us with a valuable meditation on the nature of that ongoing pattern of discernment which we are called to make between what is the case and what seems to be the case. In Christian terms this

---

14. Iris Murdoch, 'On "God" and "Good"', in *The Sovereignty of Good*, Routledge & Kegan Paul, 1970, p. 66.

meditation might appropriately be understood in terms of the distinction between costly grace and cheap grace, between the deep enfolding reality of the Trinity, the knowledge of a God who shapes our path, and the busy chatterings of our attempts at self-justification. Our attempts at self-justification seem so often to be so much more immediate and larger than life because they are the creation of our own imaginings, something which we impose on reality. Like Job before the whirlwind, we are called to silence, to rest in the facts, such facts which can never be of our own making and can only be experienced as pure gift. As Ignatius of Antioch reminded the church in Ephesus as he journeyed towards martyrdom in Rome:

> This work of ours does not consist in just making professions, but in a faith that is both practical and lasting. Indeed, it is better to keep quiet and be, than to make frequent professions and not be ... what He (the Christ) achieved even by His silences was well worthy of the Father. A person who has truly mastered the utterances of Jesus will also be able to apprehend His silences and thus reach full spiritual maturing, so that his own words have the force of actions and his silences the significance of speech.[15]

The frequent sifting through the daily tapestry of our experience provides an increasing awareness of the immediacy of God's presence in our lives. We are called to dwell in the present: both anticipation and anxiety prevents our perceiving the new and locks us into ourselves. We need to be in touch with those experiences which give us energy and to be more wary of those things in our life which diminish such energy. Where we are empowered, there we find God. All too often we wish to preserve our own picture of the world and to impose this picture on the reality around us. We escape into fantasy and provide ourselves with a script, as it were, which allows us to rehearse the agenda of our past hurts and let them provide an interpretative framework for our manipulation of future encounters. In this sense what we call sin is always in our hands, a turning in upon ourselves; it is something inevitably and uncompromisingly predictable.

---

15. Ignatius of Antioch, Letter to the Ephesians, 14, 15, in *Early Christian Writings*, Penguin Classics, 1968.

We are to be reconfigured in the image of God by incorporation into *the* image of God who is Christ. 'Through him we travel to him', says Augustine in his great work, *On the Trinity*.[16] Our path as Christians is from grace to glory, from faith to sight:

> But the image which is being renewed day by day in the spirit of mind and in the knowledge of God, not outwardly but inwardly, will be perfected by the vision itself which will then be after the judgement face to face, but now is making progress through a mirror in an obscure manner.[17]

Our journey into God is also shaped by the grace-filled pattern of the sacraments that enfold the lives of Christians and lead us to encounter God's true self. 'What was visible in our Redeemer was changed into a sacramental presence.'[18] In the Eucharist we are taken up into the pattern of the life and death of Christ and experience the reality of Christ's presence in a unique way. The Eucharist, bread broken for a new world, is the sign and expression of the church's unity with Christ and with one another, her commitment to the poor and the pledge of the life to come.

The God who reveals God's very self is both the ground of our salvation and the means by which that salvation is realised. This is the point which the Anglican–Roman Catholic Committee of the USA makes in suggesting that the search for full communion expressed in Christ's high priestly prayer calls for:

> a unity which shows forth the relationship between the Father and the Son in the Spirit, so that the world may see the glory of God revealed in the relationship of his disciples with one another.[19]

The living out of our vocation to participate in the divine life which is the mystery of the Trinity is thus the origin, the possibility, and

---

16. St Augustine, *The Trinity*, translated Edmund Hill, New City Press, New York, 1991, bk 13.24.

17. St Augustine, *On the Trinity*, bk 14.25.

18. St Leo the Great, *Sermons*, 74.2, in P. Schaff and Henry Wace, *Letters and Sermons of Leo the Great, The Nicene & Post-Nicene Fathers of the Christian Church*, Second Series, T&T Clark, Edinburgh, 1997, vol. 12, p. 188.

19. *ARC Document VII*, Dec. 1969, quoted in Joseph W. Witner & J. Robert Wright, *Called to Full Unity, Documents on Anglican–Roman Catholic Relations*, Washington, 1986, p. 40.

the goal of all our human relating, mundane though at times this experience seems to be.

It has been the argument of this book that we discover life's grounding in the mystery of God as we grow in sensitivity to those experiences which enable us to taste of joy, of wisdom and of sacrificial love. In a world scarred by the structures of sin, to live as Christ will be inevitably met by rebuff, indifference and pain: where we go, Christ has gone before. We are called to act in a way that allows us to celebrate the grounding of our existence in that communion, within whose embrace our lives are experienced. This demands that we attend to the constantly shifting pattern of reflection and response which forms the context of our prayer and the pattern of our action. It is all too easy to be all talk, to be full of good ideas. We must give our own flesh and blood to this believing, so that we may become a healing, challenging and liberating presence for those who touch our lives.

I have tried to show in the preceding pages that the study of Christ is not a matter of amassing information, increasing our knowledge of facts, but a deepening of insight, a quickening of the attention to the people and world that is taking shape around us. It is a living out of his presence. The human being is created as the image of God: 'For the glory of God is a human being fully alive and the life of a human being is the vision of God.'[20] As we sift through the daily tapestry of our experience, we gain an increasing awareness of the immediacy of God's presence in our lives. We are called to dwell in the present; both anticipation of the future and anxiety about the past event prevent our relishing the present moment and diminish our horizons. Whenever we find God in our lives, even in the darkest and most painful of experiences, there we are empowered. Here is the vision that we must live out in the communities in which we find ourselves. This is Christ in our world today.

---

20. St Irenaeus, *Against Heresies*, bk 4, 20.7 in Alexander Roberts and James Donaldson, *The Anti-Nicene Fathers*, vol. 1, T&T Clark, Edinburgh, 1996, p. 490 (I have edited the translation).

Jesus Christ: History of Interpretation

Taking its cue from Lessing's (1729–81) famous saying: 'Contingent truths of history can never prove necessary truths of reason. That is the horribly wide ditch which I cannot cross, often and earnestly as I have made the spring,'[1] there has been a tendency in nineteenth- and twentieth-century (mainly Protestant) scholarship to emphasise the discontinuity between *Jesus* and *Christ* leading to a choice between one of two paths: to pursue either the 'Jesus of history' or 'the Christ of faith'.

This has led to a further, not always healthy, distinction between what is often termed a christology from the side of God and christology from the side of the human. The former is also known as a christology 'from above' when discussion of the person of Jesus Christ starts from the point of view of language about God, using words and phrases such as Lord, Saviour, the one who forgives sin. Here the stress is on the divinity of the Word who has become flesh (Jn 1:14). This contrasts with a christology 'from below', when the starting point for discussion is the humanity of Jesus, using words such as Friend, Rabbi, Leader. Here the stress is on the exaltation of Jesus (Acts 2:22–24).

1. Adolph von Harnack's *What is Christianity?* (1899–1900)[2] regarded dogma as divisive and so focused on the person of Jesus who preached of our common Father and taught a message of love uncontaminated by doctrine which we are called to imitate. He argued that the simple gospel message had been corrupted by its association with the complexities of Hellenic

---

1. Gotthold Ephraim Lessing, *Theological Writings; Selections in Translation with an Introductory Essay*, by Henry Chadwick, London, A. & C. Black, 1956, p. 55.
2. Adolph von Harnack, *Das Wesen des Christentums*, 1900; Eng. trs., *What is Christianity?*, Sixteen Lectures Delivered in the University of Berlin during the Winter Term 1899–1900, Williams & Norgate, London, 1901.

(philosophical) thought. This approach tends to drive apart Jesus from Paul's interpretation of him, and stresses inspiration rather than incarnation.

This is the path of liberal Christianity, which had developed in different ways in the late-nineteenth and early-twentieth centuries:

> the *life-of-Jesus school* (Johannes Weiss, Wilhelm Herrmann): grounding faith in the powerful and inspiring personality of Jesus to which the Christian is related either by imitation or Christ-like trust in God.
> – Jesus as an ethical teacher; the quest of the historical Jesus.

> the *history of religions school* (Gunkel, Wrede, Bousset, Troeltsch): understanding religion not as a series of doctrines or timeless truths, but an experience rooted in a community expressed in terms of cultic or mystical experience, setting Christianity in the context of the unfolding of other near eastern religions (Egyptian, Babylonian, Hellenistic); this highlighted the role of the community and tended to eliminate the decisive event of Christ himself.

Such views were undermined by the rediscovery of the *eschatological context* of the New Testament (Albert Schweitzer, *The Quest of the Historical Jesus*, 1906, Eng ed., 1910; *The Mystery of the Kingdom of God*, 1925).

2. Rudolf Bultmann (1884–1976), and others, also challenged these developments by developing a theology of proclamation, which claimed that history can never guarantee faith, so we must turn away from the person of Jesus to the figure of the preached Christ, the saving message preached in the community.[3] Bultmann's starting point is God in Christ redeeming humanity: our call to decision before God and God's free forgiveness:

> What then is meant by *christology*? It is not the theoretical explanation of experiential piety; it is not speculation and teaching about the divine nature of Christ. It is proclamation; it is summons. It is the 'teaching' that through Jesus our justification is achieved, that for our sakes he was crucified and is risen

---

3. 'Faith is a response to the Word' (Rudolf Bultmann, *Faith & Understanding*, SCM, London, 1966, p. 278).

(Rom 3:24f; 4:25; 10:9; 2 Cor 5:18f). At the moment when this is proclaimed the hearer is summoned. He is asked whether he is willing, in the light of this fact of Christ, to understand himself as a sinner before God and to surrender himself and all that externally he is and has, to take the cross of Christ, and at the same time to understand himself as the justified one who shares the new life in the resurrection of Christ.[4]

The opening line of Bultmann's *New Testament Theology* argues that: '*The message of Jesus* is a presupposition for the theology of the New Testament rather than part of that theology itself.'[5] He goes on to marvel:

The great enigma of NT theology, *how the proclaimer became the proclaimed*, why the community proclaimed not only the content of his preaching, but also primarily Christ himself, why Paul and John almost wholly ignore the content of his preaching – that enigma is solved by the realisation that it is the fact *that* he is proclaimed which is decisive.[6]

Bultmann does this by:

- the development (with others) of a groundbreaking approach to the New Testament suggesting that the New Testament was shaped by the preaching of the early church and has its primary context here in *the early community*;
- a method of *form-criticism* allowing identification of the units of gospel tradition and their primary context in the preaching and catechetical needs of the early (Hellenistic) community, which merely looks back to the life of Jesus himself (his error was [perhaps] to overestimate the role of the Hellenistic church and Gnosticism in contributing to the formation of the gospels);
- reasserting the significance of interpreting the Christ event *eschatologically* rather than as a mystical experience; but this, in turn, is disassociated from history;
- a process of '*demythologising*' – i.e. reinterpreting the thought world of the New Testament in terms of the existentialist thinking of the early twentieth century: a life or death call to decision.

---

4. *Faith & Understanding*, p. 277.
5. Rudolf Bultmann, *Theology of the New Testament*, vol. 1, SCM, London, 1952, p. 1.
6. *Faith & Understanding*, p. 283.

'[Bultmann] made unescapable the question that lies at the heart of any understanding of primitive Christianity – the question of how the transition from Jesus to the church was made.'[7] Barrett goes on to say: 'The teaching of Jesus is New Testament theology when it is transposed out of its pre-crucifixion setting and placed where it can be seen in the light of the resurrection. For this reason we may be glad of all the modifications – even if they amount to historical falsifications – that entered the tradition in the course of its transmission.'[8]

This is the path of neo-orthodoxy (Bultmann, Barth, etc.) which denies the possibility of the quest of the historical Jesus. Here is a dogmatic, Pauline Christ founded on the mystery of the incarnation and redemption.[9]

3. This position is challenged by scholars like Oscar Cullmann who tried to reassert the historical significance of eschatology, noting the tension between the 'already here' of the Christ event and the 'not yet' of its final consummation (*parousia*), which marks the life of Christians (*salvation history*).

4. Bultmann's students tried to heal the rift between the Christ of faith and the Jesus of history by initiating a *new quest for the historical Jesus* (Bornkamm, Käsemann, Ebeling).

'The task of Christology is in fact no other than to bring to expression what came to expression in Jesus himself.'[10]

5. Modern scholarship (especially in America) puts the historical Jesus back in the centre of the picture, emphasising once

7. C.K. Barrett, *Jesus and the Word*, T&T Clark, Edinburgh, 1995, p. 221.
8. C.K. Barrett, *Jesus and the Word*, p. 249.
9. The somewhat overlooked, early twentieth-century English theologian, P.T. Forsyth comments: 'His legacy was neither a truth nor a collection of them, nor a character and its imaginative memory, but a faith that could not stop short of giving him the worship reserved by all the past for God alone. And what caused this? What produced this result, so amazing, so blasphemous to Jews? It was the cross, when it came home to them by the resurrection through the Spirit … It was the Christ who was made sin for them in the cross that became for them God reconciling the world to himself', P.T. Forsyth, *The Cruciality of the Cross*, Independent Press, London, 1909, p. 15.
10. Gerhard Ebeling, *Word & Faith*, SCM, London, 1984, p. 304.

again what we might learn from the life and teaching of Jesus himself, reasserting the Palestinian rather than Hellenistic setting of the gospels. See, for example, the work of E.P. Sanders, *Jesus and Judaism*, Fortress Press, Philadelphia, 1985; *The Historical Figure of Jesus*, Penguin Books, Harmondsworth, 1995; J. P. Meier, *A Marginal Jew*, 3 vols, Doubleday, New York & London, 1991–; 'Jesus', in Raymond E. Brown, Joseph Fitzmyer & Roland Murphy, eds., *The New Jerome Biblical Commentary*, Geoffrey Chapman, London, 1990.

6 Catholic thought, though influenced by this discussion, and often lining up more with views akin to Cullmann, has tended never to accept the extreme positions, holding together the person of Jesus the Christ (Schillebeeckx, Ratzinger):

> His existence is thus his word. He *is* word because he is love. From the cross faith understands in increasing measure that this Jesus does not just do and say *something*; that in him message and person are identical, that he always already is what he says … The apparent re-interpretation here – in Matthew 25 – of the christological confession of faith into the unconditionality of human service and mutual help is not to be regarded … as an escape from otherwise prevailing dogma; it is in truth the consequence which arises from the hyphen between Jesus and Christ, and therefore from the heart of christology itself.[11]

---

11. Joseph Ratzinger, *Introduction to Christianity*, Burns & Oates, London, 1969, pp. 152–4; see also pp. 44–154.

Further Reading

Anthony Baxter, 'Chalcedon, and the Subject in Christ', *Downside Review*, vol. 107, no. 366, January 1989, pp. 1–21.

Benedict XVI, *Jesus of Nazareth*, Bloomsbury, London, 2007.

Jean-Noël Bezançon, Philippe Ferlay & Jean-Marie Onfray, *How to Understand the Creed*, SCM Press, London, 1987.

Marcus J. Borg, *Jesus: A New Vision*, Harper & Row, 1987.

— *Jesus in Contemporary Scholarship*, Trinity Press, 1994.

— *Meeting Jesus Again for the First Time*, Harper Collins Paperback, 1995.

Raymond E. Brown, *The Community of the Beloved Disciple*, Paulist Press, New York, 1970.

— *The Churches the Apostles Left Behind*, Paulist Oress, New York, 1984.

— *An Introduction to New Testament Christology*, Chapman, London, 1994.

— 'Aspects of New Testament Thought: Christology', in Raymond E. Brown, Joseph Fitzmyer & Roland Murphy, eds, *The New Jerome Biblical Commentary*, Geoffrey Chapman, London, 1990.

Robert Butterworth, 'Has Chalcedon a Future?', *The Month*, April 1977, pp. 111–17.

Henry Chadwick, *The Early Church: Pelican History of the Church*, vol. 1, Penguin, Harmondsworth, 1967.

The Catechism of the Catholic Church, Veritas, Dublin, 1994, accessed on the internet at www.scborromeo.org/ccc.htm

The Catholic Encyclopaedia (1907–1914) accessed on the internet at www.newadvent.org

F.L. Cross & E.A. Livingstone, *The Oxford Dictionary of the Christian Church*, Oxford, 1997.

C.H. Dodd, *The Founder of Christianity*, Collins, London, 1971.

Joseph A. Fitzmyer, *Scripture & Christology: A Statement of the Biblical Commission with a Commentary*, Geoffrey Chapman, London, 1986.

Gustavo Gutierrez, *A Theology of Liberation*, SCM, London, 1974.

Roger Haight, *Jesus Symbol of God*, Orbis Books, New York, 1999.

Monika Hellwig, 'Jesus, Saviour and Son of God', in Michael A. Hayes & Liam Gearon, *Contemporary Catholic Theology: A Reader*, Gracewing, Leominster, 1998, pp. 234–50.

Elizabeth A. Johnson, *Consider Jesus: Waves of Renewal in Christology*, Crossroads Publishing, 1992.

— *Quest for the Living God: Mapping Frontiers in the Theology of God*, Continuum, London & New York, 2007.

Dermot A. Lane, 'The Doctrine of the Incarnation: human and cosmic considerations', in Michael A. Hayes & Liam Gearon, *Contemporary Catholic Theology: A Reader*, Gracewing, Leominster, 1998, pp. 209–33.

Enda Lyons, *Jesus: Self-Portrait by God*, Columba Press, Dublin, 1994 (a section of this book, 'His own Person or Divine Puppet', in included in Michael Hayes & Liam Gearon, *Contemporary Catholic Theology: A Reader*, Gracewing, Leominster, 1998, pp. 251–8).

John McDade, 'Jesus in Recent Research', *The Month*, December 1998, pp. 495–505.

John P. Meier, 'Jesus', in Raymond E. Brown, Joseph Fitzmyer & Roland Murphy, eds, *The New Jerome Biblical Commentary*, Geoffrey Chapman, London, 1990.

C.F.D. Moule, *The Origin of Christology*, Cambridge, 1977.

— 'Punishment and Retribution', in *Essays in New Testament Interpretation*, Cambridge University Press, 1982, pp. 235–49.

— 'The Theology of Forgiveness in ibid., pp. 250–60.

— 'Retribution or Restoration?', in *Forgiveness & Reconciliation*, SPCK, London, 1998, pp. 41–7.

Jacob Neusner, *A Rabbi talks to Jesus*, McGill–Queens University Press, Montreal & Kingston, 2000.

Albert Nolan, *Jesus before Christianity*, Darton Longman and Todd (DLT), London, 1977.

G. O'Collins, *Christology*, Oxford University Press (OUP), Oxford, 1995.

— *Jesus: a portrait*, DLT, London, 2008.

— *Christology: a biblical, historical and systematic study of Jesus*, OUP, Oxford, 2009.

G. O'Collins and E. Farrugia, *A Concise Dictionary of Theology*, Edinburgh, T&T Clark, 1977.

José A. Pagola, *Jésus: An Historical Approximation*, Convivium Press, Miami, 2009.

Jaroslav Pelikan, *The Christian Tradition*, vol. 1, *The Emergence of the Catholic Tradition (100–600)*, University of Chicago Press, Chicago, 1971.

Thomas P. Rausch, *Who is Jesus? An Introduction to Christology*, Liturgical Press, Collegeville, 2003.

Alan Richardson, *A Dictionary of Christian Theology*, SCM, London, 1974.

Alan Richardson & John Bowden, *A New Dictionary of Christian Theology*, SCM, London, 1983.

E.P. Sanders, *The Historical Figure of Jesus*, Penguin Books, Harmondsworth, 1995.

Eduard Schweizer, *Jesus*, SCM, London, 1971.

Jon Sobrino, *Christology at the Crossroads*, SCM, London, 1978.

Juan Luis Segundo, *The Liberation of Theology*, Gill & Macmillan, Dublin, 1977.

Stephen Sykes, *The Story of Atonement*, DLT, London, 1997.

Geza Vermes, *Jesus the Jew*, Collins, London, 1976.

Frances Young, *The Making of Creeds*, SCM, London, 1991.

H.A. Williams, *True Resurrection*, Mitchell Beazley, 1973.

Margery Williams, *The Velveteen Rabbit* at www.writepage. com / velvet.htm

Edward Yarnold, *The Second Gift*, St Paul Publications, Slough, 1974.